2022 CONSUMER TREND INSIGHTS

First published in the Republic of Korea in February, 2022 by Miraebook Publishing Co.

Inquiries should be addressed to
Miraebook Publishing Co.
5th Fl., Miraeui-chang Bldg., 62-1 Jandari-ro, Mapo-ku, Seoul
Tel : 82-2-325-7556 / email : ask@miraebook.co.kr

www.miraebook.co.kr(blog.naver.com/miraebookjoa)
Instagram.com/miraebook
Facebook.com/miraebook

ISBN 978 89 5989 702 5 13320

2022
CONSUMER
TREND
INSIGHTS

Rando Kim · Miyoung Jeon · Jihye Choi · Hyuang Eun Lee · June Young Lee
Soojin Lee · Youhyun Alex Suh · Jung Yun Kwon · Dahye Han · Hyewon Lee · Yelin Chu
Translated by Heejin Koo · Proofread by Michel Lamblin

미래의 창

Authors

Rando Kim (김난도)

Rando Kim is a professor in the Dept. of Consumer Science (DCS), Seoul National University (SNU) and the head of Consumer Trend Center (CTC), SNU. As a specialist in consumer behavior and market trend analysis, he has written more than 20 books including *Trend Korea* series, *Trend China*, *What Consumers Want*, and *Luxury Korea*. He has also written essay books, *Amor Fati*, *Future and My Job*, and *Youth, It's Painful* which have sold three million copies in 14 countries. He has conducted research projects about consumer needs finding, new product planning, and market trend probing for Korea's major companies like Samsung, LG, SK, CJ, Hyundai Motors, Amore Pacific, Lotte, Fursys, Nongshim, and Coway.

Miyoung Jeon (전미영)

Miyoung Jeon currently works as a research fellow in the CTC, SNU. She worked as a research analyst at the Samsung Economic Research Institute. She obtained her BA, MA, and PhD degrees in Consumer Science, SNU. She wrote her Ph.D. dissertation and subsequent articles about purchasing behavior and consumer happiness. She received 'The Best Publication Award' from the Korean Society of Consumer Studies in 2008. She is interested in tracking consumer trends in Korea and China as well as big data analysis for new product development and industrial applications.

Jihye Choi (최지혜)

Jihye Choi, Ph.D. in Consumer Science from DCS, SNU, works as a research fellow at CTC. She has participated in many consulting projects with Korea's leading companies such as Samsung and LG, and gives public lectures on consumer trends. She currently teaches consumer behavior and qualitative research methodology at SNU. She contributes many articles and columns to major Korean newspapers and media.

Hyang Eun Lee (이향은)

Hyang Eun Lee is an associate professor in the Dept. of Service Design Engineering, Sungshin Women's University. She has a master's degree in Design Management from Central Saint Martins in London, England and a Ph.D. in Design from the Graduate School of Arts, SNU with a dissertation: "A Study on the Process Model Focused on Experience: Centering on Experience of a Designer Transformed into Intuitive Insight." Her main area of research includes UX trends and user psychology, as well as design and consumption trends. She is working in research and development as regards to innovation in government and corporations.

June Young Lee (이준영)

June Young Lee currently works as an associate professor in Sang-Myung University. He received a doctorate degree in Consumer Science, SNU. He received 'The Best Paper Award' in *The Journal of Consumer Studies*. He worked as a senior researcher in Life Soft Research lab at LG Electronics. He is a laboratory chief of Consumer Research Center in Sang-Myung University.

Soojin Lee (이수진)

Soojin Lee has completed her BA, MA, and Ph.D. course in Consumer Science, SNU. She has been a senior researcher at CTC since 2015. Prior to joining the center, she was a stock market reporter on Maeil Economic TV. As a contributing researcher, she is conducting a number of consulting projects with clients about consumer trends. She won first prize in the Korean Academic Society of Financial Planning symposium. Her studies focus on consumer trends, consumption culture, and family economics.

YouHyun Alex Suh (서유현)

YouHyun Alex Suh graduated from Central Saint Martins College of Art & Design Textile BA (Hons) in London, UK. She received an MS degree from the Graduate School of Culture Technology, Korea Advanced Institute of Science (KAIST), specializing in design management and consumer behavior. She currently is senior researcher at CTC, and a Ph.D. candidate at SNU, specializing in data-driven trend analysis.

Jung Yoon Kwon (권정윤)

Jung Yoon Kwon is a PhD candidate in Consumer Science, SNU and is currently a senior researcher at CTC. She academically explored the changes in consumers' lives caused by technological change through her master thesis, "Consumer Happiness and Social Comparisons on SNS in Experiential and Material Purchases." Her interests include rapidly changing modern society, its impact on consumer cultures, and various research methodologies to capture them.

Dahye Han (한다혜)

Dahye Han received a BA in Psychology, SNU and an M.A. degree in Consumer Science, SNU. Currently, she is doing her Ph.D. at SNU and works as a researcher in CTC. With her masters thesis, "A Study on Consumer Emotion Changes in Online Clothing Purchasing Process," her research interests focus on consumer behavior, trend analysis, and consumption psychology.

Hyewon Lee (이혜원)

Hyewon Lee has worked at Dasan Book and Kakao Page Corp. for over 15 years. She has an MA degree with her thesis: "Comparative Analysis of Age Effect, Period Effect and Cohort Effect - Focusing on Consumer Perception Toward CSR." She is currently interested in quantifying consumer behavior, especially generational theory or cohort analysis in the digital media environment.

Yelin Chu (추예린)

Yelin Chu received an M.A. degree in Consumer Science, SNU. Currently, she is attending a Ph.D. program and serves as a senior researcher at CTC. Her master's thesis was about "A Study of Consumer Experience on the Online Education Service with Conditional Tuition Refund." She is interested in analyzing big data to distill insights from unstructured data, and in deriving further meaning from participant interviews through qualitative research.

Consumer Trend Center, Seoul National University

Consumer Trend Center (CTC) was established in 2004 to analyze rapidly changing consumer trends and has announced "ten trend keywords" every year since 2007. CTC has done collaborative research with numerous business firms and also offers educational programs on analyzing consumer needs. CTC plans to be incorporated with the consulting firm, "The Trend Korea Company," which specializes in trend forecasting, generation studies, marketing, and new product/service development.

Preface

We have published our *Consumer Trend Insights* since 2008, summing up Korea's annual consumer trends with keywords. In each of those 14 years, the books have proudly ranked 1st place on the domestic bestsellers list – a measure of support from our avid readers. We are confident that the keywords highlighted in our *Consumer Trend Insights* series are not merely an analysis of the Korean market, but universal trends that reflect the global market. We deemed it was high time to provide our global readers with a snapshot of the social changes in Korea and have published English versions since 2019. This is our third English translation in the series.

As I write this preface in December 2021, the COVID-19 pandemic continues to ravage the world since its first appearance at the tail end of 2019. Still, we are not without hope. Some in the medical community believe that the Omicron variant may well be the beginning of the end for the stubborn virus. The development of oral antiviral treatment may be a game changer that will allow us to contain the raging spread within manageable levels as an endemic. As we kick off the year 2022, the question to which we are all desperate to seek an answer is: "Will consumer spendings and other consumer trends revert to pre-COVID-19 levels, once the virus becomes endemic?"

To cut a long story short, the answer is "no." There are varying reasons for changing trends. On top of the obvious pandemic and social distancing measures, factors such as advances and shifts in the economy, society, politics, culture, and technology can turn the tide; therefore, even if we see the virus recede, it would be far-fetched to say that time will rewind to reflect our pre-coronavirus times. We further need to keep in mind that the pandemic persisted for more than two years. According to his "Acculturation Model," linguist John H. Schumann stated that it takes at least two years for one to come to terms with a new cultural environment. Even though consumers were initially unfamiliar with the rapid changes and had to endure inconveniences in the past two years, they have had sufficient time to become accustomed to the "new normal."

We now face a fresh set of trends. As predicted in last year's edition, the pandemic did not cause trends to change direction but rather hastened the way they unfolded. The year 2022 will see accelerated shifts and transitions, which will entail that we make even more rigorous preparations. And once the market settles into a more discernable pattern, companies that have managed to overcome the crisis and succeeded in pivoting their businesses will likely take on more aggressive strategies to expand their market share, moving to acquire cash-strapped rivals who have fallen behind. The trend of "winner takes all" will only intensify as the outbreak dies down. The year 2022 will likely see a series of battles for survival to determine the predators and the prey. How we counter the various trends that come in the aftermath of the pandemic will decide whether we emerge as roaring tigers or mewling kittens.

In the past 14 years, our *Consumer Trend Insights* have outlined keywords to represent the following year's trends, with the first letters of the key phrases forming an acronym that represents the animal of that year in the Chinese zodiac. For example, 2020 was the Year of the Rat, hence our acronym of the year read "MIGHTY MICE," while that of 2021, the Year of the Ox, was "COWBOY HERO." The acronym for 2022 is "TIGER OR CAT," which fittingly describes companies who are at the crossroads to either take a tiger's leap or cower like a scaredy cat.

It gives me great pleasure to acknowledge those who have helped us with this book. First of all, I am grateful to the voluntary trend hunters "Trenders Nal" for collating useful trend artifacts, which has helped to define our ten keywords.

I particularly want to thank Heejin Koo for her translation and Professor Michel Lamblin, Professor Na Yuri, and Hyo Won Yoon for their proofreading. The translation process was a tough challenge as the original Korean text uses many newly coined terms in the Korean language that requires cultural context. Despite many issues, they made succinct translations and interpretations within a time constraint. I would like to express a special thanks to CEO Euihyun Sung and the staff of Miraebook Publishing Co., who encouraged me to release an English version of the book. Lastly, I want to thank my co-authors who have generated great ideas and drafts of trend keywords. Publishing this book would not have been possible without their dedication and hard work

As previously outlined, 2022 looks to become Year One of a post-pandemic paradigm. What we should focus on is not reverting to what was but rather looking straight ahead, hoping for a fast recovery. The market and its consumers have learned and familiarized themselves with new techniques during the past two years. And no doubt they will face challenges in learning new ways to become more comfortable in a more unfamiliar territory. The key to survival in the post-COVID-19 era will depend upon how quickly we respond to new trends and how appropriate those responses will be.

German philosopher Friedrich Nietzsche wrote, "That which does not kill me makes me stronger" in his 1889 discourse *Twilight of the Idols: How to Philosophize with a Hammer*. We have endured two years of a long-drawn-out global pandemic and managed to survive. 2022 is a year that will see us stand stronger.

Rando Kim
Professor, Department of Consumer Science
Seoul National University
Seoul, January 2022

CONTENTS

Transition into a Nano Society

Korean society is becoming more fragmented. The community is breaking up into individuals and being scattered like grains of sand. Individuals then disintegrate further to a point where no one knows each other's name. We call this trend towards infinitesimal fragmentation the "Nano Society." The issue has repeatedly emerged as a continuous problem since the age of industrialization, but never more so than in recent years, emerging as a major driving force that is accelerating change in our time.

The trend of the Nano Society is often at the heart of recent changes around us, directly and indirectly affecting societal changes described in our chapters on "Rustic Life," "Like Commerce," "Routinize Yourself," and "Healthy Pleasures." The impact of the Nano Society trend can be largely broken down into three features. Firstly, as a popular saying goes, "Today's trend is that you cannot define my trend," implying a shift wherein trends are becoming more microscopically segmented. Secondly, as the individual becomes wholly responsible for his or her success or failure, labor has become even more fragmented, with people more willing to take on independent contracts, or gig work. And thirdly, families are disintegrating, with their functions becoming more commercialized and thus leading to industrial segmentation including that of retail and social infrastructures. Following its three-phased analogy of "grain of sand," "hashtag," and "echo chamber," the Nano Society tends to split up, band together, and amplify. The Nano Society is also one of the causes behind the "corona blues." We need to nurture empathy, widen our range of serendipitous experiences, and enlarge collective humanism; in other words, we individuals must establish a sense of identity with the whole human race in order to respond to these "Nano Society Blues." Under this megatrend – the Nano Society – the Republic of Korea, with its presidential elections slated for 2022, stands at the juncture of division and alliance.

"*I'm glad we have fewer office dinners due to COVID-19 restrictions.*"

Rigorous social distancing protocols have limited many aspects of our daily routines, and yet there are those who have welcomed the opportunity to focus on themselves. According to a study conducted by job search platform Saramin사람인 of 1,549 people on the pandemic-induced hourly restrictions, 48.1 percent replied that they are "satisfied." Those in their 30s saw the largest portion of positive responses at 51.8 percent. The biggest reason for their contentment was that they did not need to spend time at unnecessary after-hour company dinners (60.8 percent). This is in stark contrast with the older generations who used to say that company dinners were the highlight of their workday. COVID-19 may have altered much of our daily routines, but ironically for some of us the virus has also handed back time to us. It is a testament to the shift in our society from a community-based culture to a more individualistic culture.

"I think the store owner has begun to recognize me. It may be time for me find another hangout."

This is from a post that drew a lot of "likes" in an online community frequented by millennials and Gen Zers. They find it awkward when owners of a café or a restaurant start recognizing them, and then don't want to frequent the establishment anymore. They feel their anonymity has been penetrated and feel the burden of even the slightest bit of curiosity or interest directed their way from a stranger. In an age where it has become the norm to cover up with a mask and only reveal one's identity through a mobile number, even the lightest of hellos from the owner of a favorite hang-out feels like crossing a line. The modern world has become a society where people feel that being recognized by store-keepers is bothersome and gatherings with colleagues are uncomfortable as the community becomes more fragmented and individuals are scattered like grains of sand.

Consumer Trend Insights 2022 dubs this trend the "Nano Society," in which Korea is gradually segmenting itself into infinitesimal units. "Nano" is a unit prefix that means "one billionth," often used in atomic or molecular measurements. It implies that society can no longer maintain communal ties and has become fragmented, like molecules breaking down into atoms – that is, communities into individuals. Social atomism is nothing new. We explored the trend of society focusing more on the individual in keywords from previous editions, such as "No One Backs You Up" in 2017 and "Being Myself" in 2019. The reason why we chose the more radical term "Nano Society" this year is because the intensity of the trend has increased and has emerged as a major driving force accelerating change in our times.

"Today's trend is that you cannot define my trend."

This best sums up Korea's latest trend. "Trends," which used to be defined as a majority collective opinion that has a certain duration, are now showing signs of fundamental change. The scope of a trend's following has grown narrower as the trend's duration has shortened. People no longer "go with the flow" of a popular trend – they wait for a trend to branch out into smaller offshoots and spinoffs, like tributaries of a main river. As the sense of "we," traditionally based on one's peers and reference groups, is quickly being restructured into one based on tastes and preferences, in a Nano Society trends are becoming even more multilateral and diverse, changing at a whirlwind pace.

Such turmoil in the market has made it even more difficult to respond appropriately to change. Both public and private sectors are finding themselves at a loss as they face the challenge of identifying consumer preferences. Their analysis of consumer tastes has shown such diverse segmentation, which is updated online in real time and leads to information overload. The wealth of data has only bred sparse analysis. The same can also be said in corporate management, which has led to a great deal of confusion on whether to focus on online operations or maintain offline businesses, or confusion as to how much inventory one should even maintain. A surge of trend-related literature has taken over the bestseller lists at bookstores, a sign that the world is becoming increasingly more difficult to predict, like a buoy bobbing aimlessly in a vast ocean.

The atomization toward a more individualistic society has been attributed to COVID-19 and advances in mobile phone technology, but those are hardly the only causes. The Nano Society follows a gradual long-term trend and is also in itself a megatrend. It lies at the root of recent changes around us. As Koreans walk past one another, hiding behind their masks in an era of "Every man for himself," is this social fragmentation another crisis, or is it a new opportunity? Let's look at the implications of the Nano Society.

Three Facets of the Nano Society

In what ways can fragmentation appear in an individual? Modern people in a Nano Society tend to (a) split up into tiny pieces, (b) band together within similar crowds, and then (c) echo each other and amplify their voices. We will use the analogy of "a grain of sand," "hashtags," and "the echo chamber," to describe each of these features, respectively.

1. A grain of sand: Breaking up into pieces

Modern people living in a hyper-connected society of today are breaking up and scattering like grains of sand. Margaret Thatcher said the following in 1987 while serving as Prime Minister of the United Kingdom.

There is no such thing (as society)! There are individual men and women and there are families, and no government can do anything except through people and people look to themselves first.

- Prime Minister Margaret Thatcher,

in an interview with weekly magazine *Woman's Own* (1987)

Such remarks emphasized the importance of the individual's role in a country. And it still holds true in Korean society in 2022.

The phenomenon of scatterings of grains of sand is evident in changes in Korea's basic family unit. According to Statistics Korea, there were more than 6.6 million single-person households, making up 31.7 percent of all family units in 2020, attesting to weakened family ties and an "outsourcing" of the role of families as more and more members of society lived by themselves. Family dinners were no longer group gatherings that brought family members together, but were replaced by instant food from convenience stores, while major and trivial family events could now be managed with a few swipes on a smartphone. The dissemination of the family structure, the smallest social unit, has only deepened individualism in our society.

This also applies to the classroom. Schools, where socialization usually began among students from similar backgrounds, are also breaking up. With online classes being the norm during the pandemic, schools have passed on the knowledge but have lagged in providing the vital interactions between classmates to form relationships. This is especially true in colleges and universities, where extracurricular activities used to be as important as lectures, contributing to an extreme type of individualism during the pandemic. The students who began their college and university lives in 2020 and 2021, the so-called "Class of COVID-19," have never had the experience of going on welcome trips (or "Membership Training (MT)," as it's called in Korea) organized by the older students of their departments, or of going to a university festival or event – in fact, most haven't even met their fellow classmates in person. The pandemic has inhibited normal interpersonal relationships and allowed only the "self" to exist.

2. Hashtag: Banding together

Humans are social animals. During a natural disaster, such as an earthquake or a snowstorm, the most fatal situation is being completely isolated, and rescue workers do everything they can to locate those isolated victims. No matter how much you value your solitude, no matter the advances in technology, and no matter the restraints the pandemic has laid on one's interactions with others, people still seek connection. The question is "How?" As people find it more difficult to hook up at bars or clubs to "seek casual relationships" (or "seek natural encounters자만추: 자연스러운 만남 추구," as is commonly used and abbreviated in Korean) during the era of COVID-19, young people are actively downloading apps for marriage matchmaking agencies and for blind dates to "seek artificial encounters인만추: 인위적인 만남 추구." Such changes can be explained in the same context: as non-face-to-face contact becomes the new norm, forming a relationship through artificial means, despite the constraints of quarantine protocols, is clear evidence of how important it is for people. In his book *Phono Sapiens*포노 사피엔스, Professor Choi Jae-boong of mechanical engineering at Sungkyunkwan University, dubs such people "app-type humans." Millennials of today widely and freely seek shallow, open relationships that they can easily turn 'on' and 'off' as needed, just like the apps they download to manage their social life.

And the way these "app-type humans" meet also differs

from the past. Get-togethers are based on shared tastes. At a time when the needs of the individual outweigh the cohesion of a community, there is added emphasis on personal preferences rather than group identity. A group that defines itself with a trivial TMI, or "too much information," such as "A Gathering for People Who Dislike Cucumbers," is one such example.

This attests to the emphasis on personal preferences over and above concerns for which group one belongs to. In other words, in traditional society an individual may have found one's identity within a peer group. However, in a Nano Society, the ego is shifting according to personal tastes. As the traditional sense of "we" fades, it is replaced by a restructured trend that follows one's various preferences. Traditional ties through family, hometown, and alma mater are being replaced by a high degree of online connections based on the more variegated tastes and preferences shared by people to form a unique group. The individual is also showing complex signs of fragmentation and re-editing according to various preferences. In other words, a person can also become subdivided, breaking down and recombining in diverse ways.

"Tagnity," a pormanteau of "hashtag" and "community," is a way in which millennials and Gen Zers express their tastes and preferences by introducing products or services that they like or support. Millennials and Gen Zers enjoy games that allow them to express and best represent themselves, such as MBTI personality tests, "This or That" games, and preference-choice knockout rounds, and then come together to share the results with hashtags. The Comeet-store커밋스토어 is one such entrepreneurial result stemming from a community of common tastes and preferences, as the content-commerce platform features products often used or recommended by online influencers in the fields of beauty, fashion, and lifestyle. YouTube playlists titled "Sometimes like a calm lake때로는 잔잔한 호수처럼" or "A random song played on the way back home made my commute picture perfect무심코 튼 노래에 퇴근길이 근사해져 버렸다" prompt listeners to imagine more than just the song itself. The YouTube channel "may i choose a song for u?네 고막을 책임져도 될까?," for example, drew 380,000 subscribers in just a year and a half. Such music curation channels become a conduit for its creator and its subscribers to share their emotions and sensibilities beyond the music.

As one can see, relationships in the Nano Society no longer focus on which school you went to or where you work, but rather seeks to form ties on- or offline with those sharing similar tastes or pursuits.

3. The echo chamber: Resonating with like-minded people

Since groups that have similar preferences often share

information about what they may like, they often serve to corroborate each other's tastes. If the media and online platforms can take the lead in offsetting such biased clustering of like-minded individuals, thereby ensuring diversity and understanding of one another, the concept of a community of shared preferences would be able to have a positive effect on society. Unfortunately, the surge of diversity has fostered a culture of accessing only what one wants to see, rather than what one ought to see, or what would be beneficial for one to see, as most online media, including YouTube, Facebook, Twitter and TikTok, base their searches on "likes" and "recommendations" that reflect the tastes and preferences of the user.

The information that used to be "delivered" to us is now sifted and "selected" for us. The consumer who ultimately has the right to choose is, ironically, limited to communicating only with people with similar views, and ultimately ends up not being able to hear any opposing viewpoints. In the end, the person comes to believe that they were right, and that everyone else is of the same opinion, too. We call this the "echo chamber effect."

This echo chamber effect is even more prevalent in the political realm, where choices must be made between one party or another. Supporters of each camp only talk among themselves and echo back at each other, making claims that grow more drastic each day. They tend to look on those with differing opinions as "hostile forces," caging themselves off in their own personal "silos." A "silo" usually refers to a sealed cylindrical tower or building used to store grain. In an organization, the term is used to describe a lack of proper communication between offices or departments, or when isolation and conflict deepens between groups. Politicians are often tempted to lock voters in silos to use as their electoral base. This is because a negative strategy of binary oppositions is often quite effective. However, we will need to tear down the walls of these silos – both within and without – to establish an arena in which healthy public debate can take place to build a more resilient community.

The Nano Society: The Immediate Cause of Changing Trends

We have pointed out that the Nano Society has been the root cause of recent changes in social trends. In this year's edition of *Consumer Trend Insights*, it has affected other trends such as the "Rustic Life," "Like Commerce," "Routinize Yourself," and "Healthy Pleasures." Details of these trends will be made clear in their respective chapters. Still, we can identify three major impacts on market trends: (a) the microscopic segmentation of trends, (b) the fragmentation of labor, and (c) industrial segmentation.

1. Microscopic segmentation of trends

*Mr. Trot*내일은 미스터트롯 was a reality-survival music show on TV Chosun that swept the nation in 2020. The popularity of Lim Young-woong, who grabbed top honors, seems to have no bounds. Meanwhile, BTS, the world's biggest boy band, launched numerous singles in 2021 which made their Hot Shot Debuts atop Billboard's Hot 100 Chart. So how many BTS songs would fans of Lim Young-woong know? And vice versa: how many songs by Lim Young-woong would the millions in the BTS ARMY be able to sing along to? Herein lies the difference from the past when music charts were equally dominated by the relatively new sounds of first-generation K-pop idols H.O.T., as well as the more traditional vocalists in the "trot" genre, represented by legends such as Na Hoon-a. Granted, the generation gap still existed, but fans of both genres at least knew the titles of the songs that featured on the *Weekly Top 10*가요톱10 show. Even with a more diverse media, including those online and on cable channels, each generation is barely aware of the famous singers and their songs that are popular among other generations. Regardless of your affinity for the music of Seo Taiji and Boys, everyone in Korea could hum at least the opening lines of their song 'I Know난 알아요.' Sadly, the trend of a slimming cross-generational overlap implies that there is a lack of relatable artists or songs and attests to the reinforced trend of limitation and exclusivity.

Such tendencies are prevalent across all aspects of the cultural field. *Be My Daughter*내 딸 하자 was a show on TV Chosun, popular among middle-aged and elderly viewers, with ratings of 6.8 percent, a tremendous feat for a basic cable network. And yet, many people in their 20s, who are not considered the show's main demographic, have never even heard of the title. On the other hand, the older generations are not familiar with programs like *LOUD*라우드 or *Kick a Goal*골 때리는 그녀들 on SBS, which mainly drew a following of those in their teens and 20s, with 5.8 percent and 7.0 percent in average ratings, respectively. This is due to changes in the media environment. In the past, when all families gathered at the end of the day to watch a television show, there were common denominators in national and cultural codes. In a modern society where most people view content through over-the-top (OTT) streaming services or media platforms of their choice, that common denominator has diminished.

The short lifespan of buzzwords or trending terms also implies that generations are not keen on sharing their humor code. Normally, neologisms tend to last for a long period of time once they catch on and spread among a large group of people. However, relatively new slang words are now fading away more quickly, and the pool of shared popular terms is getting smaller. And looking at Konan Technology's lists of top ten neologisms of 2019 and 2020 among teenagers reveals that there is no overlap of words from one year to the next.

As diverse communities churn out their own sets of new slang words and lingo, their terminologies and definitions are only accepted and used by those within their individual groups. Groups may have become diverse, but communication among these groups seems to not exist.

2. Fragmentation of labor

We live in an age where each of us are responsible for our own successes and failures. As the role of the community shrinks from society to family, and then from family to the individual, each person's survival strategy becomes even more intense. YouTube is rife with channels specializing in investment strategies, with jack-of-all-trades sharing their tips on how to hold down multiple jobs. This is evident in the so-called "Money Rush" trend in which efforts to diversify one's source of income is closely linked to one's attempts to survive a fragmented society. Conversely, those who are exhausted by such trends seek a "Rustic Life" in the tranquil countryside.

In his groundbreaking work *The Tyranny of Merit: What's Become of the Common Good*, political philosopher and Harvard professor Michael Sandel asks the following questions: "Does everyone have a truly equal opportunity to compete for desirable goods and social positions?" and "Are the winners of globalization justified in the belief that they have earned and therefore deserve their success, or is this a matter of meritocratic hubris?" A Nano Society that offers no guarantee of fairness has driven us to fierce competition and, at the same time, has left us dispirited. This is one of the basic reasons why people across all generations are so sensitive about the issue of fairness. The assertion that one can do or become anything is also accompanied by inevitable anxiety that one could also become a failure. The greater the scope of freedom, the heavier the weight of responsibility, leading to excessive self-assessment.

In the Nano Society, the workplace is no longer a fixed arena but is also becoming a temporary space to gather and then disperse. In truth, the average number of years spent at a single workplace for a Korean worker stood at 6.8 years in 2020, relatively short in terms of other OECD nations. The anxiety one feels over the loss of a permanent place of employment has given birth to contractors and freelancers who rely solely on their labor abilities. These are so-called platform or gig workers. As working hours diminished during the pandemic, the number of people who divide their day into shifts to work multiple jobs has increased. Despite its controversial nature, gig work is becoming a means for modern people to ceaselessly search for new work opportunities, all while their concept of a lifetime of regular work has been shaken at its foundations.

Mobile apps such as "TalentBank," a platform that matches companies with experienced professionals and consultants, "Kmong크몽," a freelancer search platform, and "Soomgo숨고," a service and marketplace platform, have seen a surge in users seeking gig work and freelance jobs irrespective of general daily services or specialized fields. Delivery is one area to which anyone can easily apply, bringing an influx of those willing to shuttle meals or goods not just by car and motorbike, but even by bicycle, scooter, or foot.

"Bae Dateu배다트," a Korean portmanteau for "delivery배달 and diet다이어트," is an online community that caters to those seeking to earn some cash on the side while trying to lose some excess bodyweight. Its more than 110,000 members share routes and shortcuts for walking deliveries, upload evidence of actual revenue, and even post tips for effective ways to lose weight while on the job. Many have even added comments saying that for them these deliveries are not arduous labor but have now become part of their daily routines that improve their lives.

However, there's a flip side. Students taking on part-time delivery jobs, or the emergence of diverse contract workers such as YouTube creators, software engineers, and data scientists, have weakened the forum of communication. The corporate-based mutual interest between employer and employee of the past was clear. With the advent of such a wide range of gig workers, this interest becomes just as varied and gets tangled up. Their work demands may clash and lead to conflicts between members of a gig work forum and ultimately cause cracks in their social cohesion. The fragmentation of labor ultimately intensifies responsibility and, in some ways, isolates the individual. It in turn causes workers to believe that the workplace cannot guarantee a lifetime career and forces them to become preoccupied with expanding their abilities. Entry into a Nano Society is intensifying like an endless Möbius strip.

3. Industrial segmentation

The dissipation of social communities – families in particular – has led to a rapid restructuring in social infrastructure and retail to meet the relevant changes and needs of single households. Convenience stores have recently shown dramatic growth as they help resolve some of the inconveniences of single life. Revenue at the nation's top three convenience store chains during the second quarter of 2021 outpaced that of the three largest hypermarket chains for the first time since the Ministry of Trade, Industry and Energy began compiling such data 25 years ago. Not only that, the top three convenience stores' dominance lasted for three consecutive months. This attests to a clear preference for simple goods, such as ready-to-eat meals like lunch boxes and triangular gimbap, as well as products packaged in smaller units, sold in smaller stores that are closer to home, all in line with the increase in single and two-person households across the nation. Such spending trends are clear among millennials and Gen Zers: according to convenience store chain CU, customers in their teens, 20s, and 30s made up 69.1 percent of their total clientele.

Other factors that accelerated social atomism are the advances in delivery services. The Korean word for "family식구" literally means "mouths that gather together and share a meal under the same roof." However, the growth of delivery services, especially in the restaurant sector, has lessened the need to share a meal. Menus limited to Chinese food, chicken, or pizza are a thing of the past, and virtually any dish is available with the press of a finger. Colleagues used to queue up in front of famous eateries during lunch hours, but as people became more used to eating by themselves and restaurants began to deliver single portions, it became the norm to use delivery services to order food rather than spend time out of the office. The phenomenon is not restricted to meal deliveries. Coupang쿠팡 and Market Kurly마켓컬리, which offer overnight deliveries of fresh produce and ready-to-cook meal kits, have instilled the idea in consumers that it is far more convenient, less time consuming, and even cheaper to order fresh and processed food products online. Almost all products are now available for purchase online, with most of them ready for swift delivery.

We can even detect underlying changes in the industry.

As retail and manufacturing structures become more accommodating for individual shoppers, a new retail paradigm in which consumers take the lead in the process of planning, designing, and distribution is emerging. As the "direct-to-consumer (D2C)" retail structure becomes a reality, nano-scale custom-tailored production is now possible. For example, one can now order a size 6½ shoe for the right foot and a size 7 for the left. This can lead to more eco-friendly production in which there is no unnecessary waste or leftover resources. Such advances in technology can also have a positive effect on global issues such as climate change and pollution caused by excessive or lopsided spending.

Background to the Emergence of the Nano Society

In his much-touted 2014 work *Sapiens: A Brief History of Mankind*, Israeli historian Yuval Noah Harari points out how Homo sapiens was able to become the dominant race, emerging as the victor some 200,000 years ago over the physically superior Neanderthals, because Homo sapiens learned the importance of sharing myths and beliefs. The strength of the community was the impetus behind the survival and evolution of humankind. As we've passed the agricultural and industrial revolutions, the role of the community has begun to rapidly diminish in the 21st century. Moreover, Korea was traditionally an agricultural-based community. However, its transformation into an individualistic society is faster than in any other country.

It is rare to find a home in which a large family gathers in front of the television at the end of the day, watching the news or a K-drama. No longer can we find colleagues sharing the latest in-house or celebrity gossip around the water cooler or in the rec room. The hours spent at home may have lengthened, but each family member spends most of the time staring at his or her mobile phone. The "we" that gathered in front of the television scattered into each of their smartphones. We don't necessarily have to share our thoughts with friends about TV programs that we enjoyed the night before because we can chat about it with other people watching the show on social media while watching in real time. This suggests that our collective culture may be dying out.

Polish sociologist and philosopher Zygmunt Bauman dubbed the inconsistent society of today a "Liquid Modernity" in his 2000 work of the same name. He claimed that unlike traditional society of the past, when control and fairly accurate prediction was possible, modern society is unstable and indeterminate in nature, losing credibility in the public domain – in other words, credibility in the government, in organizations, and in each other is waning. COVID-19 is the last straw. As the term "social distancing" implies, people have been intentionally distanced from one another. As we have previously outlined, Homo sapiens is fundamentally an empathetic being. In fact, human facial features evolved with detailed facial muscles and wider sclera – the whites of the eye – to maximize empathetic expressions. However, in an age where all of us must cover up our faces with masks, it is difficult to feel a sense of camaraderie. The latent fear of infection has driven us to extreme isolation.

Outlook and Implications
— The need to expand empathy among fragmented individuals

Signs of the emerging Nano Society have been evident throughout the world ever since the industrial revolution. American sociologist David Riesman, together with his colleagues Nathan Glazer and Reuel Denney, postulated in *The Lonely Crowd: A Study of the Changing American Character*, a perennial bestseller since it was first published in 1950, that individuals in American society have become completely isolated, solitary beings, and at the same time, have become part of a massive crowd in pursuit of a similar lifestyle that lacks a unique character. Such analysis provides crucial insight to understanding today's modern society.

We have dubbed the depression that sprang from COVID-19 the "corona blues," but the malaise stems less from fear of the virus itself than from an individual's isolation. As society becomes highly advanced, personal contact and intimate get-togethers tend to die down. This is because even though all individuals may be part of a massive organization, they still find it difficult to form relationships with or gain acceptance from others. Numerous studies have shown that the rate of depression rises among members of a society as that society becomes overall more individualistic. COVID-19 is playing the role of a catalyst for the virus, and the situation has become dire. The number of daily average suicides in South Korea reached 37.8, equivalent to 24.7 people per 100,000 every year, topping all OECD countries. The issue is prevalent among the younger generations, especially women, bogged down by an excessive form of individualism as "death by loneliness" runs rampant. Its negative impact may be severe, but the Nano Society is not an issue we can easily change or overcome. As previously stated, it is an empirical trend and an inevitable result, rather than a question of right or wrong. What is important is that we properly recognize that we are shifting to a Nano Society and correctly understand the changes entailed to effectively counter these changes. So, what should we do during these corona blues days?

We should begin by fostering a sense of empathy. It is inappropriate to shut oneself up in a silo and simply conclude that another group, one which I don't know or understand, is absolutely "wrong." They may be "different," but not "wrong." We took the example of communities that one belongs to, but this may also apply to generational gaps in the family or within the corporate structure. It is problematic for the older generations to tell youngsters, "We never used to do it like that." One must always keep in mind that socioeconomic conditions of today differ from those of the past when the two generations grew up. The same applies for younger people, who tell the older generations "We don't do it like that anymore." Dismissing or undervaluing others' experiences or views is inadvisable. One must accept the values that helped thrust one of the poorest nations in the world through an industrial miracle, ultimately putting Korea on the map as a force to be reckoned with. Understanding and relating to the differences is the first step in creating the requisite synergy in a Nano Society.

The second step is to realize the joy of serendipity. Big data and artificial intelligence tend to confine us in an echo chamber of algorithm-induced feedback. And to break this feedback loop and make new discoveries, we need to intentionally throw things into the mix that may go counter to our own tastes and preferences. For instance, if you obtain news only through browser portals or through YouTube, then you get to read only stories that appeal to your tastes.

When obtaining information through more objective sources, such as the newspaper or TV/radio broadcasts, in which editors pick and choose stories for their audience, you encounter a wide range of views which will provide a more balanced perspective. Even if nano preferences continue to diversify within a fragmented nano group, those small preferences still need to be mixed and matched in various ways.

Technology does not provide the answer to everything. It may be convenient, but it also strips us of certain things. Social media changed the way in which we communicate, and hyper-individual technology based on big data changed our perspectives. Such advances act as an effective guide, and yet their efficacy diminishes opportunities for relatable common-denominator interests. The onboard GPS system may inform the driver of the shortest and fastest route between point A and point B, but it may also erase even the most familiar of roads. Such "highway paradoxes" or "GPS paradoxes" are metaphors for the dilemmas brought on in our age of technological excess.

Easy access to information based on recommendation algorithms generated by big data has ironically caused gaps and differences between individuals and groups to deepen. In their 2006 book, *Peripheral Vision: Detecting the Weak Signals That Will Make or Break Your Company*, Professors George Day and Paul Schoemaker of the Wharton School, University of Pennsylvania, coined the term "peripheral vision" as applied to the business realm. Peripheral vision literally refers to the ability to partially view what is outside the central area of focus. However, in the corporate world it refers to the ability to identify and interpret the minute details and signals around you and to respond appropriately. Only when companies or individuals accept the rapidly shifting trends and markets in the world with an open mind can they capitalize on the opportunities and flourish.

The ultimate pursuit for our society should be humanism. It is important not to view the world from the limited angle of the small group that one belongs to, but rather from a larger, wider perspective. We need to think from a regional, as well as a national perspective, and consider the public good to build a healthier community. Furthermore, we must look from an even greater global perspective – as global citizens – and consider our identity as members of a greater humanity. Climate change and its related extreme weather anomalies have alerted us to the fact that we are not just a particular group of people living at a particular latitude and longitude. We need a new awareness of our identities and engage socially as members of a new global community. Only when we try to understand one another and our environment and take the next step toward mutual growth can our Nano Society have a future.

Incoming! Money Rush

Money and investment concerns are at an all-time high. As the U.S. had its "Gold Rush" in the 19th century, South Korea is experiencing its own "Money Rush" as investors seek to diversify and maximize income. "Money Rush" is a keyword that follows in the same vein as that of the "Money-friendly Generation" in last year's *Consumer Trends Insight*. Whereas the Money-friendly Generation was focused on "flexing" its consumer prowess, those desperately seeking a Money Rush are absorbed with diversifying their sources of income through what can be called a "pipeline."

Those seeking to secure pipelines can be divided into two groups: those who take on two or more jobs, and those who actively leverage their assets, even taking on debt to invest, in order to maximize income. The reason for wanting to increase one's income is because spending expectations remain high despite one's ever-worsening economic situation. Higher consumer standards, based on one's exposure to social media, has boosted the desire for spending and yet has made it more difficult to prepare a sufficient retirement plan. The Money Rush is two-sided. As a testament to the materialistic nature of Korean society, the Money Rush trend may lead to excessive leveraging, referred to as "debt investments," or more sarcastically, "mortgaging one's soul," to obtain debt financing to secure seed investments – a risky move that could trigger a crisis in 2022 when rates are expected to surge. On the positive side, the Money Rush trend fosters in each of us a sense of entrepreneurship, awakening a need to design our own business models. In that sense, one needs to acquire the requisite expertise with which one can explore the application of competencies that can help expand one's career; in other words, one must practice personal pivoting. Money is only a means, not an end, and the Money Rush trend will become the means to one's lifelong mission of "growth" and "self-realization."

The discovery of gold in California and the western United States in the 19th century brought an influx of prospectors from all corners of the world. More than 100,000 people from the United States and from across the continent headed west in search of the mythical El Dorado in what has become known as the "Gold Rush." In South Korea of 2022, we can dub the rush of investors struggling to find further sources of income the "Money Rush." This can be defined as an effort to diversify and maximize sources of income, or "pipelines," such as taking on multiple jobs or increasing one's investments.

"Money Rush" is a keyword that continues in the same vein as "Money-friendly Generation" discussed in 2021's *Consumer Trend Insights*. Whereas "Money-friendly Generation" was a term for millennials and Gen Zers growing up in a capitalist society who had a more flexible view and approach to money, "Money Rush" refers to the gamut of trends and tendencies, regardless of generation, in which an immense interest in alternative sources of income in addition to fixed salaries is expressed. In other words, whereas

"Money-friendly Generation" described mostly a younger demographic, "Money Rush" designates more of a social phenomenon. If the Money-friendly Generation were more interested in "flexing" their spending prowess, those after a Money Rush desperately seek sources of income through pipelines. A comparison table can be found below.

Through the ages and in every part of the world, there has always been a keen interest in earning money. Still, those of us living in today's Money Rush age have special means and reasons for trying to earn money. Let's turn to the two issues of "How to earn money," and "Why we need to earn money."

	Money-friendly Generation	Money Rush
Age group	Teens and twentysomethings	Across all generations
Core Idea	Focus on spending	Focus on income
Relation to Capitalism	Natural acceptance of capitalism	Aggressive utilization of capitalism
Core Values	"Seek happiness impulsively, plan out concerns methodically."	"The bigger and more diverse the pipeline, the better."
Features	Minor savings, "flex" spending	Multiple jobs, leveraged investments

How to Earn Money:
Multiple Jobs and Investment

Let's take a closer look at the California Gold Rush. What is interesting about the era is that the big bucks were made not by the prospectors hoping to strike gold, but by businessmen who designed "business models" to earn a steady income from these hopeful gold miners: businessmen like Samuel Brannon, who won exclusive rights to gold mining tools and equipment at rock bottom prices, only to sell them at considerable profit to fortune hunters; or Leland Stanford, who laid the railway that carried the miners into the gold mines; or Levi Strauss, who sold durable denim jeans to the miners who needed them for working in rigorous environments.

The name "Levi's" will be familiar to many. The renowned Levi's Jeans brand is a by-product of the Gold Rush era. Strauss was able to make a successful model by selling these denim jeans to those who kept coming to seek their fortunes. Fast forward 150 years and "gold mines" still exist. However, they are no longer limited to specific locations, but rather spring from "ideas." The development of diverse platforms has given birth to the numerous gold mines of today. So, who will become the next Levi Strauss and design a business model that can become a steady earner?

Whereas prospectors needed gold mining equipment

back then, modern people choose not to sling buckets of muck and water from their potentially lucrative tunnels, but rather focus on how to lay the pipeline to funnel the water or other resource: in other words, they find alternative resources that can serve as additional income on top of their fixed salaries or regular income. Laying multiple pipelines is a corporate leveraging tool to diversify risk and to maximize profit, and today has become a strategy for private investors to diversify their investment portfolios.

So, how does one go about securing pipelines to maximize income? It entails generating a source of income other than a fixed salary or usual business revenue. This can include (a) additional income from temporary and irregular jobs such as part-time gigs, or (b) capital gains from interest rates, dividends, speculative profit margins, rent revenues, and other investment incomes. In other words, these can be boiled down to "multiple jobs" and "investments."

1. Multiple jobs

Multiple jobholders often take on two, three, or even four different jobs in addition to their regular jobs. These multitaskers work frenetically to complete their workloads and meet a multitude of deadlines. In a July 2021 study of 1,300 millennials and Gen Z workers, some 20 percent of respondents replied that they were taking on at least one additional job.

These multiple jobholders are called the "Slash Generation" in China. "Slash" refers to the slash symbol (/) which is often used to describe multiple characteristics or job descriptions ascribed simultaneously to a person. In China, young adults use this symbol to describe the multiple jobs that a person may hold. The most common form of a "slash youth" is one who diversifies their sources of income by working at nine-to-six jobs while selling goods on WeChat during their free time, or by editing videos and writing Web fiction and novels. This has given rise to a so-called "fluid society" in which there's no boundary between the main and side jobs, with people regarding themselves as a company that needs regular investment.

The "Multiple Jobholder" has become a trend, not only in South Korea but also across the globe. And with rapid changes in the workplace and increasingly unstable job security during the global pandemic, the Multiple Jobholder has become an aspiration for many millennials and Gen Zers. A close analysis of twenty- and thirtysomethings' social media accounts showed a marked interest in asset management, especially in the fields of investing, equities, apartments, real estate, and other means to increase one's wealth. Word searches for YouTubers, "BJ"s (what "broadcast jockeys" are referred to in Korea, or livestreamers), hobbies, part-time jobs, and after-hour work further reveal their interest in activities that help increase additional sources of income.

"Gig work" for short-term independent contractors is also on the rise. The gig worker is able to secure specific work or freelance services during afterhours or at specific times, thereby earning additional income and contributing to the so-called gig economy. Advancements in digital platforms have laid the foundation for such gig economies. One can easily find listings for simple tasks and jobs to be completed afterhours or during one's free time, yielding immediate remuneration. For example, those who often use takeout services can log onto a delivery app of their choice and see if anyone has ordered from the same restaurant from the neighborhood and act as a deliverer on their way back home, which will help them earn extra cash. And with such easy ways to earn additional funds, gig workers are willing to make the effort even if it is just for a small amount of money.

There are those who are willing to forgo their weekends and downtime to work multiple jobs for additional income; but there are also those who have created a multiple job niche making use of their hobbies or leisure activities. With a limit on weekly working hours, as well as reduced commuting hours and shorter lunch breaks due to teleworking, many have taken this opportunity to reinforce their sources of income.

One of the more active forms of leisure activity that many Multiple Jobholders have taken to in the gig economy is the creation of content on various easily accessible social media platforms, such as YouTube and TikTok. Aside from consuming investment know-how content, there are also opportunities to sell products through online platforms, such as creating audio content or digital books, and then selling them through digital channels, generating royalties through online distribution. This has also prompted a surge in digital publishing. Talented artists have taken to creating illustrations and portraits of famous K-pop idols, or even taking on commissions to create and trade handmade merchandise. Writing soundtracks, jingles, or backup tracks; baking homemade cakes and customized confections; holding personal readings of tarot cards – these and other various talents can all become sources of extra cash. Resales and crowdfunding are also pipelines that can provide additional income. Even lining up long before opening hours and then rushing in the minute doors open to grab limited stock items can become a means of investment.

2. Investments

Musicow is a service that auctions off stakes in copyright royalties for K-pop and global pop songs. The songwriter is guaranteed revenue from their rights to songs and the investor receives a monthly dividend for their stake in the song and can also expect a surge in trading profit if the song's value rises during the time of ownership. Brave Girls' 'Rollin'' which made a surprise comeback to the top of the charts in

2021, four years after its release, saw a record return on investment of 4,630 percent. Granted, the song enjoyed a rare viral popularity, but the startling gains highlighted just how effective copyright content could be as an investment vehicle. Musicow announced that it would expand its available copyrights to movies, webtoons, art, and intellectual property in other forms of digital content, and establish trading exchanges in the U.S., Japan, Europe, and other markets.

As we have seen in the case of Musicow, investment vehicles in 2021 have become more diverse than ever before. Aside from the traditional stocks and bonds, investors can now diversify their holdings in a multitude of items that are considered rare, such as Bitcoin, music, art, sneakers, and luxury brands. The Kansong Art and Culture Foundation issued non-fungible tokens, or NFTs, for the partial ownership of the *Hunminjeongeum Haerye*훈민정음 해례본, a 33-page Joseon-era record detailing how the written language of Hangeul was disseminated during the dynasty, to raise funds for the preservation of National Treasure No. 70. These NFTs, units of data on the blockchain representing ownership of unique digital items, were the first digital sale of a stake in a national treasure using the Ethereum blockchain platform. Sources close to the sale have said that more than 80 of the 100 available tokens were sold, each worth an estimated 100 million won ($85,000).

Investments in fine art have recently seen a marked increase, along with those in real estate and equities. As millennials and Gen Zers sought out lucrative investment targets, the fine art market was no longer exclusive to the privileged few but became a market for the masses. Local auction houses such as Seoul Auction and K Auction posted record bids daily, while art fairs in Seoul and Busan drew their highest ever number of visitors, with entries and art pieces selling out at every showing. The numbers speak for themselves. Total trading at eight major auction houses in the first half of 2021, including Seoul Auction and K Auction, reached 43.8 billion won ($122 million), some three times that of the same period the previous year. Seoul Auction saw total bids of 24.3 billion won ($20.5 million) in June 2021 alone, the highest monthly figure in 13 years.

There are alternative forms of art investment, such as joint purchases and fractional investments for those who are hesitant to splurge anywhere from several millions to as much as billions of won into a single art piece. The so-called "Art Tech," a Korean-specific portmanteau combining "art" and "investment technology," is especially popular among millennials and Gen Zers seeking to invest small sums into artwork in a group purchase format through Seoul Auction. The minimal sum group purchase art platform Art Together saw stakes in a joint purchase of *The Seers III* by Joan Miró sell out in 30 seconds in September 2020, while ARTn-

Art has become the hottest investment property among millennials and Gen Zers. Nonfungible tokens, or NFTs, a form of digital asset that incorporates blockchain technology, have captured the attention of many potential investors.

GUIDE's stake sale in Yayoi Kusama's *Infinity Nets* closed within a minute of opening.

Such fractional investments for those lacking seed money are now extending their reach from the world of art to the real estate market. Investors can now make minimal cash investments in apartments, shopping malls, and commercial buildings using real estate investment platform apps. Kasa, an indirect real estate investment app, is a service that allows investors to trade fractional stakes in buildings, much like stocks, using DABS, or digital asset-backed securities. In July 2021, it offered 800,000 DABS in G-Well Tower 2, which allowed investors to purchase 5,000-won stakes in a 15-story building in Seocho district in the affluent Greater Gangnam Area of Seoul. The total amount of DABS sold out in just two hours and 27 minutes.

Stock subscriptions of initial public offerings (IPOs) emerged as the hottest commodity in the securities market in 2021. As the hype grew over stocks hitting daily limits for two or more consecutive days, investors sought to snap up IPOs like they were buying lottery tickets. SK Bioscience's IPO in March of 2021 saw the highest number of subscriptions in history, reaching total margin deposits of 63.72 trillion won ($54.1 billion), as investors were giddy about its prospects for developing a domestically produced COVID-19 vaccine. Less than a month later its sister company SK IE Technology (SKIET), which makes materials for batteries used in electric vehicles, set yet another record as a whopping margin of 81 trillion won ($68.8 billion) flooded the market for its IPO subscriptions, driving investors' frenzy to a fever pitch. Some 1.86 million investors plopped down a combined 58 trillion won ($48.9 billion) in margin deposits for Kakao Bank's IPO subscription, the largest slated for the second half of the year, setting the competition at 183:1. Since IPOs tend to see marked gains in value as soon as they are listed on the market, even family members pool funds together to increase their chances of buying even one more share, and the elderly in their 70s and 80s, who find dealing with online subscriptions troublesome, visit their brokers to personally sign up for their subscriptions.

IPO subscriptions are a must for investors in their 20s and 30s, with cutthroat competition often resulting in just one available stock even with a deposit of 100 million won. This has prompted hotheaded investors to take drastic measures, such as taking out unaffordable loans to use as investment. These risk-takers believe in a strategy of taking on debt through their overdraft accounts or credit loans, and then subscribing for IPOs and paying back the loans with profits from selling the IPO stocks. The problem is of course that there is no guarantee that they will be able to secure the stock or, even if they do, that the stock will rise in value after its listing on the market. What is even more disturbing is that these extremists never want to cut their losses and abandon investing in stocks. With sky-high housing prices, they are adamant that the stock market is their only answer to living the good life as the older generations do. For them, stock investments are equivalent to "passing lanes" that have the highest potential to take them to their desired destination.

Such speculative debt is not the only problem. Financial regulators are issuing warnings daily on the constant rise in household debt. The surge in personal loans is not because people are in urgent need of emergency funding, but rather because of a prevalent view that it is okay to take out loans to use for investments. It is difficult these days to amass seed money just by scrimping and saving. This has prompted many to look at the possibility of leveraging. The term derives from "lever" and directly translates to facilitating the use of force by the means of a lever. Using a simple lever lessens the load of labor or force needed to complete a task. And such principles also apply in finance and economy.

In this case, it is not one's own capital but the capital of others that plays the role of a lever – that is, making returns using borrowed funds as leverage. In the world of finance, the "leverage effect" refers to when the total return on investment is considerably higher than the cost of the debt used in attaining said returns. If one has access to more than a certain level of capital, one can use it as leverage to reap considerable returns. The 2018 Korean Wealth Report by the Hana Institute of Finance, the think tank arm of Hana Bank, specifies that nearly half, or 48.9 percent, of people with higher incomes manage leveraged assets.

In that sense, we can easily find people taking out loans to pour into investments, with some taking extreme measures that some call "mortgaging one's soul" to secure as many loans as possible to use as seed money for investment. According to the figures released by the Financial Services Commission in August, the nation's household debt rose by 78.8 trillion won ($66.5 billion) in the entire financial sector during the first seven months of this year, up 71.6 percent from the same period a year earlier. It is also a surge of 3.3

times the jump seen prior to the pandemic during the first seven months of 2019, which stood at a mere 23.7 trillion won ($20 billion), according to the financial watchdog. Real estate trades, financing for long-term rent deposits known as '*jeonse*전세,' loans for investing in high-risk assets, business and living expense loans due to pandemic-induced cash crunches, are all some of the major reasons behind the recent surge in household debt; but what stands out among all these reasons is of course an increase in those willing to take out leveraged loans for investment purposes.

Why We Need to Earn Money: Living Standards that Fall Shy of Expectations

So, why are people so insistent on increasing and diversifying their income pipelines? Actually, we all know the answer to this question: it's because we need more money. And why do we need more? This too is easy to answer: expectations for personal spending have risen while one's immediate economic and financial conditions have in fact deteriorated.

1. Higher expectations:
There's always so much we want to buy

Recent spending trends have been unusual, to say the least. *Fortune* magazine coined the term "HENRY," or "high earners, not rich yet," almost two decades ago in 2003 to describe a subgroup of consumers with modest resources and luxurious tastes. These relatively young folk are usually highly educated with a great job that pays a substantial salary and yet often find themselves strapped for cash or unable to save up due to their extravagant lifestyles and student loan payments. This term best describes the quandary that many millennials face as they work ceaselessly, as if going round and round on a hamster wheel to maintain a certain standard of living. If they were to give up their jobs, it would mean a cease in their immediate source of income, and they would be left without any savings to fall back on.

We live in a society where even the local 7-Eleven can stock pricey bottles of wine. CU, one of Korea's top three convenience store chains, sold out 20 limited bottles of Château Latour at 1.5 million won ($1250) each, more than 10 bottles of the 1.5million-won Château Margaux, as well as the 1million won ($850) Château Haut-Brion, known as King George IV of England's wine of choice. An upscale hotel in Gangnam featured a shaved ice dessert, known as 'bingsu빙수,' on its summer menu featuring the pricey Shine Muscat as a main ingredient, famed for its sugary sweetness. Customers lined up to taste the seasonal dessert limited to 20 per day and at 98,000 won ($82) a bowl, selling out at every opportunity. Those who were lucky enough to have tasted the dish decried the exorbitant cost but did not forget

The façade of a glamorous lifestyle hides the reality of an empty savings account. These "HENRYs" often find themselves strapped for cash despite their considerable annual salaries reaching hundreds of thousands of dollars.

to take selfies and influencer "proofies," uploading them on social media.

The daily workout trend continued throughout the pandemic, sparking a boom among newbie golfers. Frankly speaking, golf is not an inexpensive sport as it involves costly sets of golf clubs, country club memberships, and expensive golf wear and gear. The young golfing crowd channeled much of their leisure spending, usually set aside for overseas trips, into their newfound pastime, seeking out hipper designs and more colorful balls as they brought a more casual side to traditional golf culture that had long been somber and formal.

As mentioned in Chapter 1, the reason for a high-end shift in spending is due to excessive liquidity in the market and severely lopsided spending triggered by an inability to travel overseas, which also led to revenge-type spending as a knee-jerk reaction to the corona blues. Whatever the cause may be, the fact remains such trends have made consumers seek out more money. Consumers who spend cash regardless of their income level or a desired product's price are called "ambisumers," a portmanteau of "ambivalent" + "consumers." The term best describes a specific group of consumers who are usually discerning and meticulous about purchases and yet find themselves ready to open their wallets as soon as they are hooked on something.

The South Korean government paid out its first tranche of emergency relief funds in May of 2021, 90 percent of which was claimed by the end of the following month. What is interesting is that much of the expenditure was on inessentials such as beef, luxury goods, and beauty products, rather than daily necessities. Using extraneous cash on choice items and small luxuries rather than on daily necessities is also another aspect of the Money Rush trend.

In fact, living standards in South Korea are higher than ever before. We need not even begin to mention the appalling standards when per capita income stood at less than $100 during the 1960s. It is even higher since the rate increase in per capita income began tapering off in the 2000s. There are psychological reasons why people seek better spending, even when consumer standards have objectively improved. The appearances and lifestyles of one's peers and reference groups as seen on social media, which serves as a kind of alternate or second life, seem colorful and exciting. These reference groups refer to social groups that serve as a benchmark or barometer that influences one's values, attitudes, and behavior. The fear of missing out (FOMO), or being left behind, creates anxiety stemming from the belief that others may be enjoying a better life as one continuously compares their life to that of others, particularly if they do not obtain, say, a certain product, or that trendy item that keeps popping up in their social media feeds.

The truth is these so-called "influencers" on social media hardly act as a standard for our lives. However, we are often inadvertently forced to compare these idealistic and fantastic lives of others on social media which we cannot hope to imitate with our meager incomes. American social psychologist Leon Festinger, renowned for his cognitive dissonance theory, states that everyone has an inner drive to evaluate one's own ability, opinion, and situation. The information that one obtains through a process that compares oneself with others often forms the basis of one's own assessments. And according to a study from the viewpoint of social comparison theory, the sense of comparative deprivation that one feels while surfing through social media affects one's level of conspicuous spending: those on social media are forcing us to endlessly compare ourselves with one another.

Someone may even feel that everyone else is successful except for them and feel left out and isolated because they are under the illusion that certain "influencers" are part of their close network of friends, when in fact they are not even acquaintances. As we upload posts of the best images or aspects of our lives that may be so far removed from who we truly are, we can sometimes mistakenly believe that these well-packaged and luxurious images of others represent their true selves. For some, however, this social media image is but one of their pipelines.

Like the Western saying, "Keeping up with the Joneses," there's a similar Korean saying: "If a crow tit tries to walk like a stork, it will break its legs." The problem is that the relative positions of the stork and the crow tit keep going back and forth, leading to a vicious spending loop, just to keep up with appearances. And such extraneous spending has massive consequences for the Money Rush. Spending can expand from simple accessories and clothing to non-materialistic items such as meals at restaurants, cultural outings, as well as stays at hotels and resorts. So many finer things to enjoy in life, so much money to earn – and yet, so little money flowing in. This is the problem.

2. Scraping by: Salary is not enough

The frank and fundamental reason for the Money Rush is economic uncertainty. The rate of surging consumer prices alone is intimidating. Surging prices of necessities such as milk, fish, eggs, and ramyeon (instant noodles) strain one's daily budget, forsaking any thought of saving up for retirement. Milk, ramyeon, and agricultural produce all jumped as of August 2021. Food prices in the second quarter shot up 7.3 percent, some 4.5 times the average for OECD countries, and the third highest among all 38 members. Initially triggered by a jump in oil prices, costs spiraled as weather anomalies, such as an unprecedented heatwave, caused shortages in agricultural harvests. And such volatility has stoked more anxiety among consumers.

For many in the middle class, the dream is to own a home. Skyrocketing housing prices have made such goals all but unattainable in recent years. Working hard, saving up, and buying a house is no longer possible in an age of record low interest rates. In fact, the rate of increase in capital income gains is outpacing that of labor income. According to Statistics Korea, the percentage increase for salaries stood at a mere 2.7 in 2020, nowhere near the alarming surge in housing prices for the year. The only recourse for a newlywed couple buying a home is financial assistance from their parents. However, not everyone is lucky enough to have parents who can afford to lend a hand when the elders themselves are faced with their own financial woes. Investment strategy, more commonly dubbed '*jaetech*재테크' in Korean, which directly translates as "investment technology," remains their only solution. Surging consumer prices, unstable job security, a world where it's "Every man for himself," and securing pipelines in addition to one's fixed income, have all become essential to stand on one's own two feet. And the Money Rush has become a necessity rather than a choice as urban myths began to spread of those who were able to quit their jobs after a windfall from, say, cryptocurrency investments.

Financial conditions have deteriorated and yet retirement age has quickened. The words and terms that saw the most searches on the internet in 2021 included "moonlighting permission겸직허가," "mukbangs," "Bitcoin," "starting up one's own business," and "early retirement." In other words, those who are seeking to secure enough seed money for investment and retire early are on the rise. Many are declaring themselves as part of the "FIRE tribe," the acronym for "financial independence, retire early." And as members of the FIRE tribe who advocate early retirement, they expound on various methods to cut down on spending as much as possible to maximize savings and shore up sufficient funds to embark on a post-career life. Their success stories have been released in the form of books and stories on online blogs, which kindled a boom in FIRE clubs around the world.

Everyone needs money to get by, and it's not just the

younger generation. As the joke goes, there are five things we need in old age: money, cash, funds, dough, and coin. So, the older we get, the more money we need. A longer life span would only be disastrous with the absence of proper financing. An aging body, weakening stamina, a duller mind, loneliness, and loss – all these issues will be amplified by a lack of money. Millennials and Gen Zers of the Money-friendly Generation who seek to "spend impulsively, but plan meticulously," are racing neck and neck along with the more mature and elderly generations in the Money Rush as the latter group seek to ensure that their golden years do not end in catastrophe.

Outlook and Implications

— Money becomes a means for "self-realization"

"In this problem-complex, money is simply a means, a material or an example for the presentation of relations that exist between the most superficial, 'realistic' and fortuitous phenomena and the most idealized powers of existence, the most profound currents of individual life and history. The significance and purpose of the whole undertaking is simply to derive from the surface level of economic affairs a guideline that leads to the ultimate values and things of importance in all that is human."
- Georg Simmel, *The Philosophy of Money*, Routledge, Third Edition 2004(1900)

Georg Simmel, who along with Max Weber postulated what became a theoretical standard in the philosophy of capitalism, outlined his philosophy on money as above. In other words, money is a "means" to attain the "purpose" of the ultimate human value. However, what has become of concern is that, in the Money Rush age, money is no longer just the "means" but has transposed itself to become the "purpose."

Such changes can prompt censure that Korean society is becoming excessively materialistic. However, as we illustrated earlier, living standards have risen while economic indicators have worsened. Our life expectancy has grown longer and yet we have little to set aside for our pension funds, all while the pandemic has worsened our economic and psychological insecurities. In such a dog-eat-dog Nano Society, managing one's own finances is a matter of survival. The question of how we can survive has become even more urgent.

As such, the implications of the Money Rush trend on society are all too clear. In a Nano Society, where the individual value becomes even more important, we need to shore up our entrepreneurship and attempt to pivot accordingly. Entrepreneurship is a businessperson's spirit to start a new enterprise based on capability and skill, or the ability to seek out new opportunities. Until now the concept was mainly restricted to the corporate sector. However, we have arrived at an era where the individual also must take on the entrepreneurial mindset, developing one's own business model best suited to his or her interests and capabilities. Paul Timmers, who began using the term "business models" in the contemporary sense, conceived the concept as "an architecture for the product, service and information flows, including a description of the various business actors and their roles; and a description of the potential benefits for the various business actors; and description of the sources of revenues." A standout business model changes the tide of an era. The endless array of platform services and YouTube content is the result of agonizing decisions by creators with entrepreneurial grit, born through their business models.

From a positive angle, the Money Rush is ultimately an attempt by modern-day people to adapt to changing times and "expand their careers." It is of course admirable to devote oneself to a single craft in this turbulent age when people are swept willy-nilly from this job to the next. However, that should never be an excuse to just repeat yesterday's work today, as a force of habit. One needs to acquire the requisite expertise, expanding one's competencies, horizons, and thus one's career; in other words, it is essential to practice personal pivoting. One also needs to take time for a period of self-reflection, learning, and personal leveraging. Ultimately, the Money Rush will become a means to our lifelong mission of growth and self-realization.

Gotcha
Power

Goods that are rare and difficult to obtain have become the latest "swag" to flaunt, standing out as unique from the slew of luxury items. We dub this ability to acquire rare goods that are usually unobtainable by mere financial means "Gotcha Power." In class societies of the past, people discretely flaunted their superior status and membership to a certain class by displaying refined etiquette and cultural proficiency, also known as "invisible ink." However, high-priced luxury brands began replacing the invisible ink signs of status and inclusion as anonymity grew amid rapid urbanization. In an era of communication through social media, Gotcha Power may be considered more of a "visible ink." Still, Gotcha Power features the innate qualities of an "invisible ink," such as its capacity to be shared and understood best among those who are "literate" in Gotcha Power. In that sense, it can be thought of as somewhere in between: a kind of "vague ink."

There are three strategies to Gotcha Power. One obvious method is to wait in line for hours to secure a product. Buyers queue up for hours ahead of opening time, even setting up tents, to then make a mad dash for the highly-sought-after merchandise. Next, we have those who depend on the luck of the draw to obtain the goods. Raffles or tickets for "the right to purchase" such items can be "won" through lotteries by those seeking to purchase limited-edition items. Finally, we have buyers who actively prove their earnestness to purchase the product.

Businesses have long recognized the trend, maximizing their revenue and adding to the hype by having increasingly sophisticated launches of limited-edition items and lines. From a business perspective the Gotcha Power trend has emerged as a powerful marketing tool, but from the consumers' perspective it could trigger overconsumption and a sense of deprivation. In an era of excess, where money cannot guarantee victory, the race is on to stand apart from the crowd.

We are entering a consumer market era where deep pockets don't guarantee a buy. In the past, out-of-reach products were usually extremely expensive goods – but all that has changed. We now often see limited-edition goods or collaboration items that are more difficult to acquire than high-end luxury brand goods. These are goods that are not necessarily affordable with just money alone. Those that are up for the challenge do not hesitate to go the extra mile to lay their hands on such items. They get in line well before dawn to nab those few limited-edition items as soon as stores open, with some even willing to send their real-time GPS coordinates to an up-and-coming *don katsu*돈까스 (pork cutlet) eatery to prove that they are waiting in the vicinity. Limited-edition sneakers are not available to just anyone anymore, with sellers requiring customers to earn the "right" to buy their wares. Collectors need to be well informed of the latest trends and releases in addition to honing their intuition and keen sense of timing to snatch up these rights. They need to develop a friendship with the store manager of the brand goods they are interested in acquiring. In other words, to those who are armed only with cash: the world is not your oyster.

Consumer Trend Insights 2022 dubs the ability to acquire goods that aren't readily available for anyone to purchase "Gotcha Power." The Korean version of this, *deuktemnyeok*득템력, originates from the gaming term "*deuktem*득템," a slang portmanteau of the words *deuk*득(得) – meaning "to obtain" or "yield" – and item템, in which games "reward" online or offline RPG players with power-up items after defeating bosses or completing challenges. The term has expanded and now is part of shopping lingo. The growing emphasis on Gotcha Power does not simply indicate an increase in hard-to-get limited-edition items, but points to the start of a market era with shifts in perceptions of rarity. Moreover, Gotcha Power is also a sign of the times, which provides a means to differentiate consumers, expanding from the mere ability to make a purchase to encompass the capacity to obtain a particular experience or limited item. In a market that weighs buyers' effort and earnestness in addition to price, how are consumers displaying their Gotcha Power? They are laying everything on the line to emerge as victors in this cutthroat Gotcha Power race.

From Purchasing Power to Gotcha Power

Norwegian-American economist Thorstein Veblen, who noted the trend of conspicuous consumption among the upper class during the 19th century, discovered a curious correlation between prices and demand of luxury goods. Usually, demand ebbs as prices of products go up. However, the opposite held true for specific items. Defying demand curves in general, the "Veblen effect" would occur in which clamor for such items rises after the price exceeds a certain level.

The driving force behind the Veblen effect is the desire to show off. This desire is fundamental to and part of human nature. German philosopher Georg Wilhelm Friedrich Hegel stated that human beings essentially seek recognition and that this is one of the most fundamental of human desires. With our self-conscious desire we are even led to a struggle for recognition, and depending on the outcome, ultimately end up in a structure of "lordship and bondage," of independence and dependence. The need to be recognized is also displayed in the form of an "economic desire." This in turn develops beyond seeking recognition from others and leads to a need to display one's superiority through the act of "acquisition, conservation, and formation" of objects, in order to gain acceptance as a wealthy and refined individual. The need for superiority then mutates to a desire to show off. Thus continues a pattern of vanity spending to fulfill the need to show off.

As Hegel's age-old insights state, humans seek to exhibit their affiliation through the products they consume. In previous class-based societies, the more affluent members aspired to show off their superior status by means of "invisible ink." This refers to a specific group of people honing their knowledge in more nuanced appreciations of music, poetry, games, dance, and etiquette, sharing them with others in affiliated groups as mutual codes of inclusion. Attending performances of the latest opera, or acquiring the proper manners in appreciating wine – these and other forms of less accessible knowledge were how they sought to discretely differentiate themselves from the other classes. "Invisible ink," then, refers to how such knowledge and training is not easily seen.

However, in the present day, it has become difficult to show off one's status merely through invisible ink. Revolutions and the collapse of the class system have led to the rapid development of urban culture, which in turn has brought about increased anonymity in current society. As a result, a desire for a more "visible ink" has emerged, and one means of fulfilling that need was high-end luxury goods. Items with exorbitant price tags that are out of reach for most people became an effective means to flaunt one's status as a member of the upper crust. The excessive pricing of such goods became a status symbol. This ultimately led to the Veblen effect of raising the demand for costly merchandise as people sought to prove their purchasing power.

The Veblen effect was evident in South Korea as well. Louis Vuitton opened its first store in South Korea in September 1984. There were only three employees when it first launched. By 2020, Louis Vuitton had topped the list of best-selling international luxury brands in the country. According to data released by the Ministry of Trade, Industry and Energy, sales of international luxury brands jumped 57.5 percent in April 2021 compared to a year earlier, exceeding revenue growth at department stores in the same period, which stood at 34.5 percent. Among the three best-selling luxury brands in the country – Hermès, Louis Vuitton, and Chanel, more commonly referred to by their collective acronym "*He-Lu-Sha*에루샤" – Chanel, which has a bigger following in Korea than in many other countries, saw its sales climb 34.4 percent in the cited period. According to market research firm Euromonitor International, total sales of luxury goods in South Korea reached $12.5 billion, or nearly 15 trillion won in 2020. This attests to the popularity of luxury brands and its market in the country in less than 30 years.

However, a collision between extravagant spending and social media has led to another shake-up of the megatrend. Consumers, who previously held exorbitant price tags as a "visible ink" that defined their social status, are seeking a new benchmark as new hurdles emerge to replace cash as the indicator of status. Previously, the ability to afford high-end goods served as a barometer to set oneself apart from others. However, that standard has shifted from financial prowess to focus more on the ability to acquire items that are nearly impossible to obtain. French sociologist Pierre Bourdieu stated that "distinction" is an inevitable result of "ostentation." As such, he observed that luxury spending becomes "an exhibition of wealth" and consequently "a source of credit."

And the way in which these new consumers set themselves apart has recently changed. If consumption previously yielded gaps that separate social classes, the classes of today do not imply a divide between the upper and middle classes. Rather, they refer to: a discerning eye that can recognize items that garner recognition from others; the work that goes into acquiring the unique item; and the ability to gather information that provides an edge to obtain the product. In other words, the "swag factor" of today focuses more on one's positioning as a trendsetter that creates and responds promptly to trends and fashion, going beyond merely flaunting one's wealth.

The rules of distinction in the class-based society of the past that focused more on hidden tastes and refinement shifted to the more visible form of luxury brands on the heels of industrialization. In a society where extravagance becomes more widespread and as people post evidence on social media of their Gotcha Power, such abilities are usually considered a form of visible ink. However, it can also be considered an invisible form in the sense that it is an ability that is more likely shared among those proficient in Gotcha Power. As such, we would like to dub this strategy of setting oneself apart by means of displaying one's Gotcha Power a

<Periodic Changes in Distinction Strategies>

	Invisible Ink Strategy	Visible Ink Strategy	Vague Ink Strategy
Period	Class-based society Inherited classes	Industrial era (advent of the nouveau riche, increased anonymity)	Era of social media (pervasion of extravagance, increased social comparisons)
Purpose of Showing Off	to display inherited status	to brag about one's wealth	to display wealth & understanding of trends
Examples	Language, etiquette, genealogy, high tastes (sophistication through a foreign language)	Luxury goods (ultra high-end brands)	Rare luxury goods limited editions, rarities
Requirements	Etiquette & Culture	Financial Power	Gotcha Power

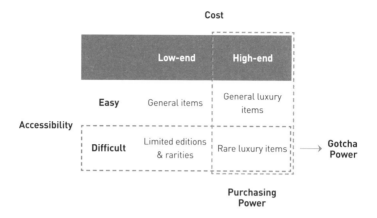

<New Index to Measure Purchasing Ability>

"vague ink" strategy, between that of invisible and visible ink. A comparison of these three concepts is listed in the table on the previous page.

Another important point is that Gotcha Power is not limited to the high-end market. It is easy to find examples of items that are not necessarily pricey but are difficult to obtain, leading to cut-throat competition. Accessibility has become a new standard for measuring consumer power, rather than pricing. The above table illustrates these changes.

In the past, as shown in the vertical Y axis of the chart, rarity of an object used to depend on purchasing ability. Nowadays, the horizontal X axis, representing accessibility, plays a key role in determining the value of the goods in question. So, in a market that requires Gotcha Power in addition to buying power, how are consumers displaying their ability to acquire hard-to-get items? Let's look at the three strategies involved in attaining the necessary Gotcha Power.

The Three Strategies for Gotcha Power

1. Opportunity comes to those who wait

At 3:30 a.m., August 8, 2021, a group of people gathered in the parking lot behind the Apgujeong Hyundai Department Store in the affluent Gangnam district to begin their long wait. One was snoring inside his pop-up tent, and another lay dozing on the bare pavement under his open black umbrella, half propped by his backpack. Most were part-time student workers who were queuing up as proxies for their clients who wanted to make the mad dash for the limited-edition Rolex watches to be launched that day. And as a cub reporter for Chosun Ilbo, I decided to join the ranks of these part-time workers in their long wait to experience firsthand the so-called "open run" race the second the doors opened.

Thus began an article written and published in a major local newspaper. An "open run오픈런" is a Konglish term that refers to the mad dash at opening hours for high-ly-sought-after merchandise at department stores and other retailers. And as lines have begun to form earlier and earlier, and wait times to grow longer and longer, "queuers" have emerged as a niche part-time job.

Waiting in line is the most obvious strategy to enhance one's Gotcha Power. When demand far outweighs the limited supply of much-coveted items, potential buyers are all too willing to endure the interminable wait to lay their hands on the goods. This is not just a wait of some 10 or 20 minutes. As the reporter describes, the line-up begins hours before stores open, with some events drawing eager and determined crowds the day before opening. In the case of Chanel, some even line up days or even a week before the launch date of an exclusive handbag, which has been the cause of numerous frantic open run races according to the relatively few boastful success stories posted on social media. This happens quite frequently for Chanel's products because there is no guarantee that a certain model stays in stock, and many open runners fail to secure a product even if they were among the first to arrive at the store. Items available for purchase may depend on pure luck, prompting collectors and afficionados to dub the race a "luck run," with jokes saying, "I don't get to choose; it's Chanel that makes the choice for me."

In light of this, some potential buyers and collectors have banded together to share tips and information regarding these runs, including what to prepare ahead of the long wait. Downloading whole seasons of dramas or TV series, movies, updating YouTube and music playlists, securing portable chargers and batteries, and setting up camping chairs and giant parasols are all par for the course. The phenomenon has also driven up hourly rates for these semi-professional queuers, earning them as much as 50,000 won ($42) for a three- or four-hour stint, far exceeding the nation's hourly minimum wage of 8,720 won ($7.36). One entrepreneur even began offering a proxy waiting service for these runs. The Open Run Godvatar오픈런 갓바타, a service that is available through social media, began operations in June 2021, providing legal work contracts for its part-timers as well as assurances for both the clients and the workers, hired only after various background checks. The proxies or "avatars" begin their queues hours before dawn outside the store in question and hand off their precious spots to clients at around 9:30 a.m., 30 minutes before they open. Second-hand trading app Karrot당근마켓 often has listings offering spots at the start of these queues, with one such spot at the head of the line selling for 250,000 won ($211).

Gotcha Power items are not limited to luxury brands. On May 21, 2021, crowds began to gather and form lines long before dawn outside SSG Landers Field, the home stadium for the Incheon-based pro baseball team. They were hoping to nab the 160 uniforms up for grabs at the Landers' official store. In January 2021, police had to respond when scuffles broke out in front of a Starbucks branch at a shopping mall in Seoul as queuers began to squabble over their spots in line while waiting for limited-edition Playmobil Buddy Set toy figurines, available only to loyal customers who had racked up enough purchases.

Gotcha Power is not just limited to goods but may also involve unique experiences. Pobangteo Don Katsu포방터 돈가스, a deep-fried pork cutlet eatery in Seoul, saw its number of visitors explode after it was featured in October 2018 on the extremely popular *Baek Jong-won's Alley Restaurant*, a reality TV show on SBS. The hoard of foodies descended on the usually serene neighborhood in northern Seoul, drawing complaints from neighbors amid increased noise pollution, cigarette smoke, and littering. The stream of complaints forced the tiny restaurant's owner to move to the island of Jeju. With a new store name, "Yeondon," the eatery remains a popular destination among tourists and local customers, with some even waiting in line overnight, armed with pop-up tents and other necessities, turning the parking lot outside into a makeshift campground. Some enterprising firms began operating a service renting out tents to those willing to wait hours ahead of opening hours in front of the restaurant. The near-endless queues forced owners to overhaul their waiting process using the mobile platform Tabling테이블링. Making a reservation at Yeondon involves the following steps:

1. Download the Tabling테이블링 App. Join as a member, with your ID certified through your smartphone.
2. Input "Yeondon" in the search field.
3. Reservations for the following day begin at 8 p.m. sharp and end quickly, so you must be alert.
4. Entering the restaurant is only possible after all members specified in the reservation have arrived.
5. Reservations are limited to those on Jeju Island after confirmation through GPS.

Here we should note the last requirement, that one must provide proof that they are making the reservation on Jeju Island at the time of booking. Such a complicated procedure is necessary for a hugely popular restaurant to mitigate no-shows. This also prohibits attempts at making reservations by proxy. This means that one must physically be in Jeju to make a booking to eat the famed dish. There have been reports of Jeju locals making proxy reservations and then selling them online, which has served as the latest twist in the drama for a bite of fried pork. And such propensity to flock toward specific merchandise, locations, or experiences has only resulted in more stumbling blocks for customers to overcome to satiate their desires.

2. Get lucky and make a grab for it!

"Luck" is another strategy to enhance one's Gotcha Power.

Frankly speaking, there has always been controversy over the fairness of waiting in line, as professional distributors and middlemen have always employed part-time workers to serve as proxies waiting in line. The average Joe or Jane can hardly afford to take three to five days off from their day jobs just to wait in line. And the system has been under constant fire as standing close together in a line violates social distancing protocols during the protracted pandemic.

And thus, the online lottery has emerged as a viable alternative. Raffles are one key example of the lottery system in which "purchasing rights" are awarded for limited-edition and other items in short supply. This may involve handing out lottery tickets to everyone seeking to make a purchase, or the vendor can even limit the number of available tickets. Some brands call these raffles "draws," as in drawing or selecting from a deck of cards. We need to emphasize once again that these draws only provide the "right to purchase" rather than a guarantee for the items themselves. In other words, one needs not only the cash but also a little help from Lady Luck to acquire the item in question. "Drops" are also another method that requires good fortune and involve the sale of limited-edition goods at a certain date, time, and specific location, which has often been used as a marketing tool to draw consumers.

Nike is a brand that actively makes use of raffles. They award raffle tickets, or purchasing rights, on limited-edition models of their sneakers, some of which are the results of collaborations with famous artists. Offers of Nike's online raffle tickets often crash their servers as collectors and buyers clamor to receive a ticket. And even if you are lucky enough to win the raffle, you are still far from succeeding in making a purchase as the company often limits the timeframe for the customer to make their purchase. The global sneaker brand held a raffle for just 30 minutes for its "Nike × Sacai VaporWaffles" at 12:30 p.m. on April 29, 2021. Winners of the raffle were announced at 1 p.m., and they had only two hours to buy the sought-after shoes. Despite the moans and groans surrounding the audacity of the sneaker brand, the company's server crashed yet again as potential buyers logged on to its website.

Other brands have jumped on the raffle bandwagon. In April 2021, E-land World, a retailer and clothing manufacturer, offered raffles on the grey "327 Lab" models of the hugely popular New Balance sneakers, handing out some 80,000 tickets. The 2020 raffles for New Balance's most globally recognized "Classic 993s," better known as the "Steve Jobs sneakers," drew an even bigger crowd with an estimated 130,000 taking part in the event.

Raffles are not exclusive to sneakers and footwear. Gotcha Power has also become a must in the IT sector, requiring hopeful buyers to grab the opportunity to buy unique editions of the latest in technology. When Samsung unveiled the latest Thom Browne editions of its Galaxy Z Fold3 and Z Flip3 smartphones in August 2021, the price tag on the limited-edition Z Fold3s stood at nearly 4 million won ($3,375), and that of the Z Flip3 at 3 million won ($2,530). Some 460,000 wannabe owners sought the unique editions, named after the iconic American fashion designer and bearing his signature red, white, and blue striped grosgrain ribbon, which was double the number that sought raffles for the Z Fold2 Thom Browne edition.

Raffles are also often used by retailers as marketing tools. Musinsa is an online shopping platform, that actively makes use of raffles to raise interest and appeal to their targeted demographics, the younger millennials and Gen Zers. The October 2020 raffle for its Dior x Nike Air Jordan 1 limited-edition High OG "Air Dior" sneakers drew some 350,000 potential buyers, its highest number ever for a raffle event. Two months later in December, Musinsa held another raffle event when rap artist Kanye West collaborated with sportswear maker Adidas to release "Yeezy Boost 350 V2" sneakers, choosing just one single winner among some 280,000 potential buyers. Looking at the figures alone, it's difficult to say whether the buyers are trying to purchase sneakers or a lottery ticket.

3. Proving just how much you care

Please wear a Nike T-shirt and Air Force 1s to apply for a raffle ticket.

These days customers are asked to prove their love for and sincerity to a brand. And this is not to purchase the rare items from the vendor, but just to receive raffle tickets that give one the right (but not the guarantee) to purchase said items. Nike has even added a "dress code" clause to its raffle system. When it held a raffle for its Air Force 1 "Para Noise" in November 2020, potential buyers were asked to don Nike shirts and Air Force 1s in order to receive tickets. Fans and collectors flooded social media with selfies dressed head to toe in full Nike gear. Only those passionate about the brand and its Air Force line were able to qualify for the raffle tickets.

Starbucks, which also has a huge, dedicated following, requires collectors of its exclusive merchandise to buy a minimum number of beverages within a specified time frame to collect online coupons (a system better known as the "e-frequency" program) to earn the right to purchase the seasonal and exclusive items. Such clauses have prompted fans and collectors to share posts and videos on the most effective way to fulfill the coffee franchise's "e-frequency" requirements, such as the "Esso Tip" in which the customer only orders espressos. Starbucks' highly popular 2021 Summer Day Cooler bag and Summer Night Singing Lanterns also caused some waves. Consumers quickly learned that buying 14 espressos, the cheapest item on the Starbucks menu, and three Vanilla Crème Frappuccinos, the cheapest among beverages listed as a mission requirement, would allow them to qualify. Bringing their own thermoses or tumblers to help further minimize costs, customers could meet the minimum requirement for the loyalty program at just 59,700 won ($50).

Having a friend on the inside also helps. Customers invest time and effort to befriend a store manager or clerk to gain the latest information, thereby learning what is left in stock at which branch or outlet, and even receiving a heads-up whenever the store is about to receive new stock. One department store official points out that many experienced clerks and managers at luxury brands keep track of each customer's tastes and preferences, how often they visit, how much they buy, their clothing and accessories, and even whether they intend to use the item themselves or if they intend to resell it. Therefore, if customers continuously display their sincerity and affection for the brand over several weeks and months, these insiders will sometimes set aside limited stock for the loyal customers, giving them an edge and enhancing their Gotcha Power.

We live in a market era in which customers are required to display their sincerity before acquiring an exclusive item. As the Korean saying goes, a thirsty person digs their own well. If I desire a certain item, others will inevitably desire it, too. We can only emerge victorious by bowing to the audacious demands made by brands and retailers in this cutthroat Gotcha Power race. After all, in a lopsided relationship, those who love the other a little bit more usually end up being more vulnerable.

Sociocultural Background to the Emergence of Gotcha Power

I'm not that worried about the pandemic. I'm more worried that I won't be able to get my hands on the model I want.

Such were the concerns of one person anxiously waiting in line to buy a luxury brand watch in the predawn hours in front of a department store in Myeong-dong's shopping district, downtown Seoul. Needless to say, the gathering throng did not heed social distancing guidelines of staying apart from one another, less concerned about the viral spread than about nabbing the products they wanted. Even amid an outbreak, competition has become fiercer in the consumer market to attain the desired items and experiences. What is the reason behind such fervor?

Firstly, as we outlined previously, the context and strategy of "swag" is changing. German philosopher and sociologist

Georg Simmel wrote in a 1904 essay that the fashions of the upper stratum of society are never identical with those of the lower; they are in fact abandoned by the former as soon as the latter prepares to appropriate them. In other words, fashion is both a means and a result of class distinction. People recognize this distinction, creating it and thereby maintaining and regenerating the balance of power. As noted previously, such distinction served as an indicator of class in the past, and that of wealth in modern times. However financial standards are no longer enough to explain consumer patterns of today. The Gotcha Power race heats up even for inexpensive but popular limited-edition goods. In the realm of Gotcha Power, the level of one's wealth is no longer an issue.

The steady pervasion of extravagance and a protracted period of a global pandemic has led to a rapid surge in prices of equity, cryptocurrency, and real estate, resulting in a larger pool of people with considerable wealth. This nouveau riche, often referred to in Korea (in English) as the "young & rich" crowd, are not satiated by simply spending an enormous amount of money. They place more value on items that others cannot easily obtain. Flexing their Gotcha Power, rather than their purchasing power, becomes the true measure of success. Moreover, in an era of social media that allows constant social comparisons between one another, boasting one's wealth has become all too common. There is a craving for unique ways to boast one's special spending abilities.

Secondly, we should note that consumers are enjoying the process of attaining the unattainable, showing off their experience on social media. They derive a sense of accomplishment by getting their hands on items that are not easily accessible. Their main targets are highly-sought-after products or services that are mostly difficult to obtain, and their restricted availability only stokes their sense of competition. For them, a successful Gotcha purchase means they came out on top in the race. Their sense of pride over "being able to get things that others cannot" makes Gotcha Power all the more appealing. They also derive an odd sense of exhilaration over the fact that they can snag items that cannot be bought, but only be attained through their Gotcha abilities, regardless of the time, effort, luck, and love that goes into a successful outcome. Social media is inundated with bragging accounts of their journey, sharing tips and skills that led to their success in the Gotcha Power race. Such posts are filled with comments such as "Congratulations!" or "I wasn't so lucky," "I am green with envy," and "It was an all-out war."

Thirdly, the surge of interest in hard-to-obtain items has created a market for these rarities, allowing them to become a source of investment. After the mad dash for luxury items or the battle to reserve exclusive limited seasonal Starbucks merchandise comes the "resale" market. Reselling involves purchasing or obtaining limited-edition goods or rarities, then putting them up for sale at a premium. The resale market has recently emerged as a valid 'jaetech재테크' investment strategy, even generating the term "Resell-tech리셀테크(리셀+재테 크)." With rising premiums on these rare items, sometimes even doubling their initial value, the market has given rise to professional traders who often try to corner certain sections of the market by hiring as may part-time workers or proxies as they can. As stated earlier, brands and vendors are adopting countermeasures to break up such unfair monopolies, but the demand for these items as a means of investment has grown even higher.

As outlined in our chapter on the Money Rush, limited-edition sneakers and brand-name items are considered a popular investment item among Gen Zers, as the public seek diverse forms of investment. High-end luxury goods may be difficult to purchase, with initial price tags on rare merchandise usually costing between 100,000 won ($85) and 200,000 won ($170). Sneakers have a solid market base: limited-edition kicks rarely see a price dip thanks to passionate collectors, both locally and overseas, propping up their value. Their profitability, or return on investment (ROI), can range anywhere between 5 percent and 200 percent. Starbucks' exclusive merchandise is among the top picks that generate the most profitability in the secondhand market. Their limited-edition Playmobil toy figurines, released in January 2021, generated 217,278 searches on the thrift platform Bungaejangter번개장터 in the three months of February to April, raising their value by as much as 1,318 percent over the cited period. And as consumers seek to diversify their "pipelines" to generate additional sources of income on top of their salaries or fixed income, obtaining Gotcha items has become part of their economic routine.

Finally, companies are catching on to the trend and are seizing the opportunity to maximize sales, fueling the craze through their sophisticated marketing of limited-edition items. Whenever a product becomes a target of a Gotcha craze, it provides a golden opportunity for its manufacturer. Therefore, many brand names have taken to limiting supplies as part of their marketing strategy. The heat is on in the Gotcha Power race as businesses tempt their consumers with promises of limited goods reserved only for them.

Outlook and Implications
— Money won't guarantee a score in the new consumer era

Be it positive or negative, the Gotcha Power trend is objectively an interesting change in that it has given rise to a new consumer culture. It is a hallmark of consumerism in the era of social media, as the means of ostentation have changed from hierarchy to wealth and finally to the Gotcha ability. For companies that need to generate revenue, the implications of the Gotcha Power trend in the market are its usage as a potent marketing tool, while concerns remain for consumers and society in general. Let's look at its inherent pros and cons.

From a corporate perspective, companies are faced with the challenge of pushing their brands and products as a lucrative lure for Gotcha Power enthusiasts. The basic approach is to release limited-edition items or to place a cap on supplies, thus maintaining a constant shortage. Still, not all limited-edition items become Gotcha goods. Not many companies can hope to emulate the top three "He-Lu-Sha에루샤" brands, where buyers turn up in droves for new releases. Nike's raffles initially drew little interest. Just 10 years ago it was viewed as a mass sports brand popular among the younger generation. It only emerged as a strong contender in the collectors' market after successive collaborations with numerous artists and other luxury brands, seeking to enhance the value of its identity and products. As a result, Nike topped the Lyst Index for the world's hottest fashion brands for the first time in the second quarter of 2021, beating out the usual champions Gucci and Off-White for the first time. It was also a first achievement for any sports brand to edge out luxury brand names for the list, compiled by the London-based global fashion platform and search engine. Officials in the sportswear sector said that Nike's unique planning and releases of special editions and raffle schemes had paid off.

Organizing special events in which customers can score limited-edition items is another effective marketing tool to generate buzz. Department stores had been faced with growing concerns that people no longer found the retailers attractive. They had been worried about a steady decline in their younger clientele, especially as millennials and Gen Zers rarely visited these high-end retailers. In that sense, the Gotcha phenomenon is welcome news for these large-scale retailers, excited about a resurgence powered by a booming Gotcha market. The Hyundai Seoul, Seoul's biggest and newest department store, caused a sensation when it announced that it would open an offline sneaker shop for BGZT Lab브그즈트 랩 on its premises, a division of thrift store operator Bungaejangter번개장터. The Shinsegae Department Store in the Gangnam area beefed up its luxury brand shops, even opening a mega five-floor spanning pop-up store for Louis Vuitton. All this points to a major shift in the core business strategies of these large-scale retailers.

However, concerns remain about the overheated competition in the Gotcha market. Experts point to "Resalems되팔렘" as the ones causing the biggest problem in the industry. These are traders who snatch up goods for the sole purpose of reselling them at outrageous premiums. "Resalem" is a mash-up of "Resale" and "Nephalem," the half angel, half demon characters from the Diablo gaming franchise who alter the balance of power in the game's universe. Resalems first emerged when Blizzard released Diablo 3 in 2012, as profit seekers hoarded the sought-after copies of the game, then reselling them at a considerable premium.

These Resalems are always on the hunt for the next Gotcha items, those that are in short supply and will likely see a surge in demand, readily employing part-timers willing to act as proxies and even making use of macro instructions that allow them to automatically execute a series of actions in the blink of an eye, giving them an edge over other hopeful buyers in acquiring rare items. Such actions often force actual users and enthusiasts to pay an exorbitant amount of money to acquire the products from Resalems. The U.S. and Canada have adopted laws that prohibit the use of macros to buy tickets with the intent of scalping. South Korea, however, has yet to adopt such laws.

There are also those voicing their concerns that Gotcha culture can cause a sense of relative deprivation. With restrictions on outdoor activities due to the pandemic, people are more dependent on social media as a channel of communication with the outside world. And when social media is full of posts about Gotcha successes, it may seem that everyone else is happy, successful, and living the good life. Everyone, that is, except oneself. In other words, it becomes all too easy to fall into a rut of fear of missing out (FOMO).

Accounts showing off their successes in snagging items that are notoriously difficult to obtain, sharing photos that prove they managed to purchase extremely rare or limited high-end goods, may trigger a feeling of hopelessness or lethargy. According to the Ministry of Health and Welfare's comprehensive review of the general population affected by mental health issues due to COVID-19 in the second quarter of 2021, the depression score, and the depression risk for those in their 20s and 30s, was found to be higher than in other age groups.

Sean "Seongjik" Lee, Adjunct Professor of Psychology at Yonsei University, points out that structural issues in Korean society are aggravating relative deprivation, and that one of the reasons may be so-called "feel-good spending가심비 소비," which is in stark contrast with "cost-effective spending가성비 소비" from which this Korean neologism is derived. A recent upsurge of depression among millennials and Gen Zers is cause for concern, and while feel-good spending may not be the primary reason for their gloom, it counts as a major contributing factor. This is because a stream of photographs and posts on social media can leave them feeling helpless and powerless.

Gotcha Power suggests changes in the market principles of capitalism, which dictates that consumers need to be provided with an endless means of distinction. Companies need to be able to maintain public interest in their products, brands, and marketing in any way possible. They walk a fine line between encouraging the public's thirst and generating negative feedback. Those who are proficient in the art of an emotional tug of war tend to gain the upper hand in relationships. Companies must also learn to maintain a similar level of tension with their customers. In an era of excess, consumers' desires to distinguish themselves from others are overlapping with sophisticated scarcity marketing strategies. The Gotcha ability of understanding the value of rare items and obtaining them has emerged as the up-and-coming consumer power in a society of ostentatious spending. The modern race to set oneself apart has begun, as money alone cannot guarantee victory.

Escaping the Concrete Jungle – 'Rustic Life'

It's hip to be rustic. The countryside is no longer a dilapidated region that has fallen behind the times. Rather, it offers a leisurely pace for city folk bogged down by the mundane humdrum of the metropolis, thereby emerging as a charming place even with its inevitable inconveniences that come part of the package. The "Rustic Life" aspires to a lifestyle that favors the countryside, offering the appeal of raw nature and the unique charm of rural areas, and bestowing a sense of comfort and serenity for city folk who often find the everyday routine a burden. Rather than completely isolating oneself in the countryside, the Rustic Life trend beckons people to seek a touch of the simple village life for a few days of the week.

Depending on how you divide your time between the city and the country, the Rustic Life can be divided into four stages: "Departure," "Stay," "Settling in," and "Taking root." Those "departing" the city enjoy their break surrounded by nature, and also create a new routine by "staying" in the countryside. People seeking to incorporate the Rustic Life in their urban routines do so by "settling in" a base from which they manage both aspects of their lifestyles in parallel, or by building farming areas or houses in the country, thereby "taking root" or residing in a new neighborhood with a fresh start to a new life.

The Rustic Life is a significant trend for both the overcrowded metropolis, densely packed with residential areas and office buildings, and for the regional autonomous districts struggling with an aging population and rural hollowing. The global pandemic has also provided an opportunity to showcase various rural areas to these Rustic Life buffs as they focus more on local regions. Local governments are seeking to take advantage of this golden opportunity to ride out their economic slowdown and reverse their declining populations. It has become imperative for them to respond shrewdly to this trend and make full use of this chance.

Zannier Hotels Phum Baitang is a premium resort in the second-largest Cambodian city of Siem Reap, home to the UNESCO World Heritage Site of Angkor Wat. The luxurious retreat rose to fame after Hollywood A-lister Angelina Jolie and her family called it home for months while she was directing the 2017 wartime drama, *First They Killed My Father*. The resort's name, which means "green village," boasts a unique scenery of oxen ploughing rice paddies and lemongrass scented meadows, rather than the typical breathtaking resort views of sea, mountains, or waterfalls. Jolie apparently enjoyed winding down from a long day's shoot with a drink on the terrace of its cocktail and cigar bar that offers such greenery and magnificent sunsets.

The glamorous superstar is not alone in choosing to end a hectic schedule with tranquil scenery over the bright lights of a big city. In South Korea, rice paddies and farmlands are also emerging as therapeutic landscapes to heal the soul. 'Onulun오느른', a YouTube channel that posts vlogs about giving up a Seoul residence to live in the countryside, saw its subscribers top 300,000 in just over a year. The YouTuber, a 30-something year-old TV producer, bought a rundown house for 45,000,000 won ($38,000) in Gimje located on the "great plains" of North Jeolla Province – a three-and-a-half-hour drive away from work. She says she made the decision because "even a haphazardly placed rock on a chair looked pretty in this area." Her videos manage to turn simple shots of a tree frog hopping about, or the rippling waves of unripe barley, into documentaries. Her video comments section is filled with messages of empathy and gratitude for the young office worker brave enough to choose a rural life: "Thank you for reviving a sentiment I had long forgotten," or "Thank you for living my dream life for me." A country life that some may find unremarkable has become an ideal for others.

No need for stunning views or extravagant interior designs. As more people living in modern society seek out their small patch of land, their own healing spot, it is becoming hip to be rustic. The countryside, contrary to what it may imply, is no longer considered a dilapidated region that has fallen behind the times. The countryside has come to offer the appeal of raw nature and the unique charm of rural areas, bestowing a sense of comfort and serenity for city folk who often find the everyday routine burdensome. These days when the urbane has become routine, the countryside has become an extraordinary locale of ideals and romance – one's own special hangout. The rustic life no longer signifies a state of reclusive isolation but rather offers a period of

YouTube Channel 'Onulun오느른', which depicts a quiet life in the country, has resonated with young adults who dream about such a lifestyle.

replenishing essential to everyone from all walks of life. Such a countrified lifestyle does not entail cutting oneself off or departing completely from the city. It does not imply that one must exile oneself from the metropolis but rather that one can aim to spend less time in densely populated towns and experience a touch of the simple village life for two or three days of the week.

"Rustic" encompasses a sense of the countryside, simplicity, and crudeness. A rustic style with regard to interior design exudes a comfortable countryside atmosphere by, for example, preserving the natural grain of hardwood furniture, or by haphazardly placing a simple rock as part of the interior decoration. It is not as classical as country or antique styles but is versatile enough to be incorporated into modern interior design, creating a "Modern Rustic Style."

"Rustic Life" symbolizes a lifestyle that leans towards a rural life and that allows people to enjoy the rawness of nature and unique charm of the countryside while injecting a sense of ease and comfort into city life.

The Four Stages of the Rustic Life

1. Departure: A visit to the countryside

The first stage, or the introduction to the rustic life, begins with a short visit to the countryside for an experience that only it can offer. A typical example is a "*countrycation* (country + vacation)" or a "*hanokation* (hanok + vacation)." This may include spending one's holiday in the countryside at an inconspicuous old house or even a traditional Korean residence known as a "hanok한옥", relishing in the unique tranquility and comfort that comes from the passage of time.

*Sangolchoga*산골초가 is an accommodation complex of standalone country homes or cottages located in a rural corner of Yeoungwol County in Gangwon Province. There are no other buildings or structures in the immediate vicinity of the complex, allowing guests to be lulled by an all-natural ASMR (autonomous sensory meridian response) of birdsongs and frog ribbits amidst the forests and mountains. It offers city folk a novel "countrified" experience akin to traveling back in time, complete with kindling fires to cook meals in large cauldrons.

Rustic travel is not limited to the choice of accommodations. In an age where finding one's location with GPS or driving with the assistance of a voice navigation system are second nature, embarking on a journey with only a paper map may prove a daunting and yet novel experience. This requires city slickers to turn off their smartphones if they want to completely log out of their usual urban lifestyle, and to take only a piece of paper from the local tourism office. Travelers can seek out hidden gems and lesser-known locations armed with maps hand-drawn by local residents, rather than tourist landmarks that one can easily find through online searches. These maps, which often invoke desire with their emotional designs, are eagerly sought after by younger travelers in their 20s and 30s who tend to regard them as limited-edition merchandise. The Jeju Tourism Organization, which sends maps through the postal service, has to repeatedly put up a notice saying they have filled their daily quota, attesting to the popularity of these paper maps.

Modern people, stifled by their dreary urban lives, often try to seek an experience that offers a chance to enshroud themselves in nature without putting too much thought into the process. This can involve spacing out while being mesmerized by what nature offers, such as the flames of a campfire, the undulating surface of water, or the rippling of grass in the wind. Locations that allow visitors to lose themselves in such alluring vistas have emerged as must-see hotspots. These are not just cafés that serve tasty beverages; they are sprawling areas often equipped with floor-to-ceiling windows, dotted with shaded seating and sofas, offering #oceanviews#바다뷰 #paddiesandfarmlandviews#논밭뷰 and #sunsetviews#노을뷰 that can be readily browsed online on social media and other platforms.

In addition to the renowned cafés with stunning coastal vistas, such as those in Busan, Incheon, and Gangneung, more cafés are cropping up inland overlooking rice paddies and farmlands. Cheongdo, in North Gyeongbuk Province, is fast emerging as a hotspot for its #paddiesandfarmlandviews#논밭뷰. The 70-odd number of cafés in the district three years earlier has jumped to 112 as of 2021. And with the influx of tourists, the Cheongdo municipal government designed a special map focusing on the 100 or so cafés in the area, which also list their unique qualities. Such café clusters, in conjunction with local landmarks, have created a distinctive tourism ecosystem.

2. Stay: Spending time in the countryside

If a short trip only leaves you wanting more, you could always opt for a longer stay. Month-long sojourns on Jeju Island, Paris, or Bali have often appeared on bucket lists for travel buffs in the past ten years or so. And you can even see the rustic trend in these month-long home-away-from-home adventures. Whereas people used to only dream about unrealistically long vacations, the month-long stays of today have become a means for rebooting one's daily routines through "self-exile," away from the hustle and bustle of the city, avoiding the better-known tourist destinations and heading to more remote areas such as Donghae, Sokcho, Yangyang, and Namhae.

And as those in their 20s and 30s have embraced the trend, unfettered by the constraints of family, they flexibly adapt their vacation durations to their work patterns and schedules, settling on living away for, say, a fortnight, or ten days. And in line with the rising interest in extended stays, platforms such as 'Mr.Mention^{미스터멘션},' which offers reservation services for long-term accommodations, has seen its revenue skyrocket fivefold in 2020 from a year earlier. Local governments have also been eager in their response. The relatively laid-back port city of Donghae on the eastern coast has redesigned its tourism resources to offer various activities and experiences to cater to those who are residing for an extended period in the area, rather than offering just one-off events. For example, the Bookstore Village along the Dongho Beach area renovated rundown houses through its communal cooperative to offer as long-term residences for young artists and urban visitors.

And as social distancing measures push more companies to adopt telecommuting during the pandemic, office workers are taking the opportunity to observe a more rustic way of life. They are breaking with traditions that limit work to the office and are now adopting a practice that combines work at vacation spots: the "workation." Japan's corporate sector and regional governments have been embracing this concept for several years. Japanese IT service provider Biglobe set up a "Workation Space" in Beppu, allowing their Generation Z employees to take three-month shifts working at the nation's southwestern resort town renowned for its hot spring baths. The company has high expectations that working in an unorthodox environment will breed creative ideas. Japanese Airlines, together with a consulting unit of NTT Data Institute of Management Consulting and the nation's largest travel company, JTB, published a study of a three-day workation involving 18 participants in Okinawa during June and July 2020. The findings, reported the following month, showed a 20.7 percent rise in productivity and a 37.3 percent decline in stress levels. And as South Korean companies move to introduce similar incentives, autonomous regions are vying fiercely to lure young office workers. The "Orossi오롯이, 하동" weekly program run by Hadong County, South Gyeongsang Province, offers a fully catered service that includes not only a shared workspace but also accommodation, transportation, beam projectors, and even a picnic set – in other words, you can come without any luggage whatsoever. Gangwon Tourism Organization, together with online shopping platform Interpark, offered a workation package that included room upgrades and extended hours for check-in and check-outs, helping boost sales for the March-May period by 25 percent from the same period last year.

The charm of country life can also invigorate the lives of children. At a time when many students were cooped up at home attending online classes, many parents opted to send their kids to receive a "country education" by attending a school closer to nature.

The Seoul Metropolitan Office of Education joined forces with the South Jeolla Province Office of Education to develop a program that sends school children from Seoul to live in rural areas for a semester or two at small-sized schools in remote villages with less than 60 enrolled students. Such small schools were allowed to continue conducting face-to-face lessons and as such were popular among parents who were concerned that their children were feeling more disassociated from their school lives, allowing them to have a break from the same mundane routines in the city and to enjoy fresh experiences every day, like running outdoors in the countryside. Another advantage with the smaller sized classes is the abundance of educational resources. Children can camp in the playground in spring, or catch shellfish and mudskippers along the beach. Such is the laid-back nature of life in the countryside.

3. Settling in:
Transitioning from a visiting holiday to a leisurely stay

The countryside has long been a symbol of one's origin and roots. Many of us have imagined ourselves wondering what it would be like if we were to go to the countryside after we retire. Such instincts to return home and even take up farming remain strong among Koreans.

According to a 2020 survey on agricultural and rural areas conducted by the Korea Rural Economic Institute, 41.4 percent of 1,500 people living in the city responded that they are planning or are willing to relocate to the countryside. Still, a complete relocation may seem far-fetched for some Koreans when considering, for example, their children's education, social networking, or social and cultural activities. So rather than uprooting themselves completely from their urban roots, they take a more balanced approach by setting up bases from which they can manage a "dual lifestyle," one of which fulfills their desire for a rustic way of life. Balancing between both worlds is best expressed by the terms "Five days in the city, two in the country오도이촌," or "Four days in the city, three in the country사도삼촌." It is worth taking note that such terms, which were trendy among the middle-aged or older generations, are now popular buzzwords for those in their 30s and 40s. There are several ways to establish bases to manage a dual lifestyle. The more mature or middle-aged generation, who are financially better off and have been preparing step by step for a life in the country, will likely acquire a country villa within a private community that is actively being developed in, say, Yangyang, Yangpyeong, or Gapyeong, or they may set up a second home in condos, apartments, or residential offices in resort areas such as Gangneung or Sokcho. Relatives and family members may also want to chip in for a long-term rental contract so they can take turns staying at the residence. Even a cabin suffices to act as a base. Farm storage units, orders of which have soared in the past few months, used to be cargo containers for storing agricultural tools, seedlings, and the harvest. These farm storage units are evolving to reflect the needs of various customers. Some are even equipped with a kitchenette or a small upstairs bedroom area. Many have windows that offer stunning views of the wilderness just outside, transforming themselves into mini villas.

Japan has long seen its share of overcrowding. MUJI, a Japanese retailer that offers a wide range of basic household goods with minimalist designs, once sold its own "MUJI Hut." As the name implies, it was not a house but a box-like abode, which was an ideal solution to serve as a rural base. It was especially well known for how nature-friendly it was, and how minimalist its features were. MUJI did not simply offer its huts at its stores but collaborated with regional centers to help resolve the issue of rural hollowing and population decline. It sought to alleviate the worsening housing issue by building MUJI Huts on lots rented from Shirahama Community Center located in Minamiboso for those seeking to have a place of their own but who were unable to find a plot of land themselves. This community center also renovated a dilapidated elementary school that had closed due to the town's dwindling number of children. On the flip side, this allowed the center to make use of the school's wide spaces, including its playground, and visitors could also make use of facilities such as kitchenettes and bathrooms that they had been sorely lacking, allowing visitors to stay for longer periods of time and helping to reinvigorate the community.

We can grasp the changing trends in camping in conjunction with the dual lifestyle. Going on a camping trip once in a blue moon keeps the task of pitching a tent – and then packing it again – a mere novelty. However, as we begin to go on more frequent camping trips, the repetition of such time-consuming labor and dealing with endless amounts of gear becomes a hassle. Camping enthusiasts are now choosing the more rational option of renting out a location to camp at for extended periods of time, or even refitting their cars so that they can sleep in them. Others are choosing "campnics (camping + picnics)," in which they don't sleep outside overnight but just rest in the shade, enjoy their picnic outing, and then pack everything up and head home for the night.

4. Taking root, nesting:
farming, building, creating an experience

The final stage of the Rustic Life is creating one's own rustic lifestyle. We are not just talking about middle-aged and elderly retirees who have uprooted their lives to come to the countryside to begin farming. We are also talking about younger generations who have decided to create their own way of life and who are quickly changing the rural landscape. Many have opened stores and businesses by renovating rundown areas and buildings, rejuvenating the atmosphere of a village that had seen better days. The township of Ansa in Uiseong County, North Gyeongsang Province, with a population of just 800, repurposed its post office which had closed operations due to population decline, turning it into a restaurant. All three partners who currently run the restaurant are in their 20s. They all met while attending a state-funded relocation program run by Uiseong County for the younger generations.

A new generation of farmers is also making a name for itself. A strawberry farmer uploading pictures of his strawberry flowers, or the owner of a vegetable stall who uploads posts of the season's produce as well as videos of him making the trendiest of dishes with his fresh veggies, are all members of the so-called "cell," or "single-person," market, adept in the ways of communicating in real-time with their customers. Such changes are even more evident in official figures. The number of households in their 20s and 30s that relocated to rural areas climbed 8.2 percent to 140,642 in 2019 from 129,913 in 2014, according to figures from Statistics Korea. Of the total, those under the age of 29 jumped by 40 percent to 64,536 from 45,797 over the same period. Mo Jongryn, Professor of International Political Economy at Yonsei University, often touted as an "alleyway economist," emphasizes the need to focus on local businesses because millennials, with their strong sense of identity, consider local spots as not just on the outskirts but as the focal points for realizing their unique lifestyles.

Building one's own house can be considered an act of taking root, or nesting. Videos of remodeling or renovating country homes, or of introducing real estate listings of country homes, are surprisingly racking up considerable views on YouTube. More and more city folk are drawn to the idea of being able to afford a house with a yard at a price with which they can hardly rent a room in the city. They dream of being able to design and build a space tailor-made for themselves, their families, and companions. And recent television programs have reflected such desires. *There's No Home for Us in Seoul*서울엔 우리집이 없다 on JTBC, shows the program's hosts and guests searching throughout the country to hunt down the home of their dreams. They even show the renovation process for some of the houses, which gives the viewer a sense of vicarious satisfaction.

The Rustic Life is not always limited to the countryside. One can always create a "rustic experience" without leaving the city. The most common example is gardening. The outbreak of COVID-19 prompted nature lovers to bring their gardens onto their verandas, with some even branching out to home farming. These would-be cultivators can grow a wide variety of vegetables, starting from entry level produce such as bean sprouts and red lettuce, moving on to more complicated ones such as lemon trees, arugula, and basil.

Background: COVID-19 Sparks a New Lifestyle

So, what has pulled the public to the countryside at a time when excessive urban development is leading to rural hollowing? One obvious reason is the global pandemic. The pastoral regions, away from the teeming masses, are often considered safe areas and relatively free from the risk of infection. And as we begin a so-called "untact" era, where we can get by with limited face-to-face contact, and where one is able to work, attend classes, shop, and enjoy one's down time from the comfort of one's home, our desire to flee the hectic chaos of the metropolis has grown even more. Yoo Hyunjoon, professor of architecture at Hongik University in Seoul, explains that many of us feel that our homes have grown smaller as they have, in a sense, exceeded their capacity by at least 50 percent due to our increased time at home. Moreover, many workers are pleading "COVID-19 burnout" as there is no separation between work and home, and as workloads become unmanageable. There has also been a surge among those suffering from the "corona blues" as they refrain from social activities. Such is the desperation and yearning for a rustic life – to regain one's health, peace of mind, and sense of safety during the age of a global pandemic.

We would like to reiterate that what COVID-19 has changed is not the overall direction but rather the pace of change. People were already adding a dash of the countryside to their monotonous routines even before the onset of the viral outbreak. Urban garden patches expanded almost 13 times over from just 104 hectares (257 acres) in 2010 to 1,300 hectares (3,212 acres) in 2018, with the number of budding gardeners and city farmers increasing at a similar rate from 153,000 to 2.12 million over the same period.

It is perhaps instinct that drives us to the countryside – that emblem of healing – to offset urban society's cold indifference. E.O. Wilson, touted as "the father of sociobiology," introduced the concept of "biophilia," which states that humans are naturally drawn to and attain a sense of stability and rejuvenation from nature. This is probably why we derive a feeling of peace when looking at the tranquil landscapes we set as our screensavers and wallpapers on our monitors. The threat of viral infection merely accelerated our spatial orientation towards the countryside.

Another reason for the increasing departures from urban areas is that the lure of city life has become weaker. The city, with its hordes and multitudes, provides a wealth of advantages, such as diverse educational opportunities, better job prospects, and agreeable living arrangements. Convenient amenities, as well as entertainment and leisure facilities, only available in densely populated areas are also part of the reason why we cannot leave these sprawling cities. Still, the appeal of the city has waned somewhat with the recent increase in non-face-to-face lessons and telecommuting, as well as the virtual shift in leisure activities that are no longer spatially bound, such as creating and watching YouTube videos or viewing shows on Netflix. A mobile shopping platform that lets you buy anything from furniture to luxury brand items, or the Baemin food delivery app that allows you to order spicy "malatang," or Chinese hot pot, with the swipe of a finger from even the most remote farming area, has further enabled more people to take the plunge and move out of the city. A vast amount of information on living the Rustic Life is easily available online and has presented the countryside as an even more appealing alternative.

A trend toward living away from the city for a month or becoming a "rustic nomad" and uprooting oneself and settling in the countryside shows a decided shift in social networking for Koreans. In a past culture where a collective mindset was predominant, it would have been unthinkable to abandon one's community, to leave behind a group of people you have shared similar interests and lifestyles. As relationships have become more diverse and no longer merely limited to traditional ties of blood, alma mater, or one's hometown, people find themselves living in a "nano society" where they incorporate themselves into a society based on their shared values. Pursuing one's own unique lifestyle is no longer peculiar but is rather in style, and it has allowed a city dweller with no ties to the countryside to move to a small village and transform themself into a local online content creator.

Separation does not imply complete isolation. A nano society entails changes in the ways we communicate and form relationships through shared tastes and interests. People nowadays have more in common with online "friends" and "followers" than with their actual neighbors. We live in a world where you can communicate with a hundred or so people with shared interests even if you live in the wilderness far removed from a town or village. The shake-up in communication channels also offers consumers who seek a rustic lifestyle with more sources of entertainment. You can go in search of a hidden gem of a house in the countryside from the comfort of your little nook in the concrete jungle, or even order freshly grown produce from a farmer who you have never even met.

Outlook and Implications
— A countryside easily accessible to anyone is key

What are the implications of the Rustic Life? To begin with, its impact on autonomous governments is considerable. About half, or 26 million, of the nation's 51.8 million population are currently crammed into the Seoul Capital Area, comprising the capital, nearby Gyeonggi Province, and the city of Incheon, with an urbanization rate of more than 80 percent since 2000. A trend toward the Rustic Life would provide a win-win for both the densely populated megalopolis as well as the sparse regional areas struggling with aging and hollowing communities.

Nonetheless, local governments should be wary about

designing projects and vaguely pinning their hopes on an influx of urbanites. According to media reports, the "Youth Mall" projects that the South Korean government ambitiously created in traditional markets across the nation since 2017 have mostly ended in failure. It was inevitable as most of these projects simply set up cafés and workshops for young artists and entrepreneurs within the markets without basic knowledge or research about the neighborhood or their target clientele, all in the vague hope that these malls would draw millennials and the Gen Z crowd. Such projects need a more strategic and methodical approach.

This begins with a "consumer-oriented perspective." As mentioned earlier, as we become more nano-centric, so too should the approach to understanding consumers and their needs. Local governments need to conduct exhaustive analyses on the demographics and lifestyles of the visitors and consumers they wish to target, which would then lead to establishing their own unique and segmented infrastructure that can help pave the road to success. Above all, they need to understand that these consumers who dream of a rustic lifestyle are not just one single segment of society, but rather a collective of individuals with different and diverse purposes. They all have vastly different expectations of the terms "rural" or "countryside." According to an analysis of search terms related to the countryside in online communities, younger consumers in their 20s and 30s looked up related terms through online content and stories, feeling vicariously sated by observing the lives of YouTube content creators and livestreamers, and taking pleasure in imagining a life in the countryside. Those in their 30s and 40s, on the other hand, were more interested in practical matters of settling down, such as housing and rental prices, state subsidies, and job opportunities, as well as specific issues such as farms, agriculture, managing a farm, and other farm-related subjects. Such subtle differences indicate they would need to take a customized approach to securing potential clients and visitors.

Local governments also need to present a more accessible countryside, both physically and mentally. In that sense, they should lower these barriers for the commitment they require from city dwellers who want to enjoy the Rustic Life, many of whom want to experience growing their own produce but who are relative newbies when it comes to gardening or farming. For these people, taking one day out of their busy week to drop by their weekend farm would not be an easy feat. Lowering the barriers and encouraging their interest would be key to the success of their projects.

Secondly, local governments must hold onto their unique identities. As markets flourish by focusing on their strengths and what makes them unique, the districts' singular charm should be able to add value to their tourism resources, specialty products, and services. These administrations need to carefully review and consider what kind of stories they wish to tell as part of their "charming districts" presentation. Pale imitations that fail to differentiate themselves from other regions, or excessive development that causes the areas to lose their unique charm, would only lead to failure – a kind of "cultural gentrification."

Thirdly, public and private sectors, as well as local communities, must join forces to help lead such projects to success. Public funding can obviously provide the "hardware" in laying the foundations for the necessary facilities. However, there are limitations on the "software," or the cultural content and programs, that can be provided. This is where the role of local communities and other entrepreneurs who provide private investment and sponsorship take center stage. A public-private partnership (PPP) becomes essential to the success of such a project.

Finally, speed is vital. The countryside may be the epitome of a slow and easy life, but such projects need agility, flexibility, and readiness. Japan, which has been agonizing over the hollowing of its rural areas for much longer than Korea, serves as a valuable lesson. The town of Shirahama, which was touted as the "Waikiki of Japan," began an all-out push in 2017 to reimagine itself as the prime destination for workations. The local government allocated public funds to provide visitors access to public Wi-Fi, including on its famed beaches, and proactively encouraged IT-related companies to send their employees there on workations. As a result, the number of monthly visitors jumped to 1,500, even during the off-season winter of 2020, from just 300 in 2019, and with one IT-related company moving its headquarters to the area.

• • •

Little Forest, a 2018 indie film by director Yim Soon-rye, tells the story of a character who comes back to live in her childhood home in the countryside, slowly regaining her spirit and vigor that she lost while living in the city. The countryside provides a wealth of seasonal food ingredients brimming with vitality, which provides a source of healing for the main character as well as the audience, unlike the barren city and its instant food. In the end, what the movie leaves the audience with is a piece of a "little forest." In Germany, every household has an allotment garden, called a *Kleingarten* or a *Schrebergarten*, each with a small cabin, patch of garden, trees, and flowers, usually located at the edge of a city, easily accessible at the end of the workday. There are some 1.5 million of these "little gardens" in Germany, with 1 in 20 Germans tending to one. Some are created as public parks and gardens. One study showed that such gardens contribute to the happiness of more than half of the nation's population. These "little forests" and "little gardens" do not attest to the modesty of their size but indicate that even if they are not grandiose, they provide comfort and small pleasures of the soul. The key to the Rustic Life is not simply living in the middle of nowhere, but rather living in a countryside easily accessible to anyone.

How we view these small pleasures is also changing. Those moments of comfort and peace of mind are the ultimate form of extravagance, or "ordinary luxury," in a world of cut-throat competition. After riding out trends such as "YOLO (You Only Live Once)," and "Small but Certain Happiness소확행," keywords covered in our 2018 edition, our day-to-day happiness has become a major public issue and a standard by which we judge whether we are properly balancing our work and private life. Not only are we trying to even out our work-life balance, but now we are also seeking a healthy balance between the urban and rustic life. The Rustic Life trend will not only provide an opportunity for a more symmetrical development for the country, but also a chance to enhance the quality of life and happiness for Korean society.

Revelers in Health –
'Healthy Pleasure'

Fitness is trending. Health has always been important, but the topic of fitness and immunity have emerged as buzzwords during the global pandemic, pushing health concerns to the fore. As the younger generations put more emphasis on taking care of their health, it has become mainstream to maintain fitness in a way that is both enjoyable and sustainable for everyone. Consumers are no longer willing to tolerate the pain of dieting and starvation for the sake of losing a few pounds to meet a set standard for health. To reflect the general view that managing health has become a pleasure, we would like to dub this trend "Healthy Pleasure." In contrast with its evil cousin "guilty pleasure," where feelings of guilt accompany one's pleasure-seeking ways, a Healthy Pleasure is a win-win wherein pleasure can still be found in healthier living. Health and fitness, which used to be considered difficult, rigorous, and laborious, is changing to become easily manageable, sustainable, and even something we can revel in.

The emerging Healthy Pleasure trend is a result of the outbreak of COVID-19 and is simultaneously in line with the view "I am the only one to look after my health" in a segmented Nano Society. In other words, health and fitness has become the epitome of self-management. The propensity of millennials and Gen Zers to value themselves more than anyone else is providing a wider base for the trend. Its dissemination has shifted emphasis from treatment to prevention, as evidenced in health management changes that are in sync with "hip" lifestyles of advanced nations. As such, the market needs to keep up with the rapidly changing pace of consumer needs with fresh and trendy approaches to fitness management, rather than maintaining mundane routines. In other words, we need to find novel strategies in response to this rising happy and sustainable trend of Healthy Pleasures.

Case #1. After a bowl of salad, I like to treat myself to tooth-achingly sweet ice-cream. You may ask why I have a salad in the first place if I'm going to have dessert, but it's okay: the ice cream is low in sugar with low-calorie sweeteners such as stevia and erythritol.

Case #2. When I'm dead tired, I check my stress levels through my smartwatch and soothe my aching neck and shoulder muscles with an electric massager. If all else fails, I play an ASMR video that helps me fall asleep. The sounds of rain, wind, or footsteps in the snow lull me into a deep sleep until the morning comes.

People choose various methods to maintain their well-being in keeping with today's trend of an enjoyable and effective health routine. At first glance, fun and effectiveness may seem contradictory. As the saying goes, "good medicine tastes bitter," and we often equate keeping fit with routine exercises and perseverance. However, recent fitness trends are focusing more on enjoyable health management.

Modern people who view health management as a form of self-improvement are concentrating more on taking care of themselves.

Taking an interest in one's health is basic human nature, and as such has been a steady trend. However, keywords of the past, such as "well-being," were more focused on detoxing or protecting oneself from harmful elements, both physically and mentally. In other words, a healthy life meant having to sacrifice fleeting pleasures, giving up on the little comforts in life. Unfortunately, such methods cannot prevail indefinitely. People inevitably seek out things that are familiar and enjoyable, and thus further distance themselves from maintaining a healthy lifestyle. People of today demand a fitness routine that does not require them to retrain themselves. They are looking for a sustaining routine that allows them to maintain their current state of fitness. It reflects contradictory human emotions such as wanting to maintain a healthy diet and at the same time indulging in sweet ice cream, or wanting to relieve anxiety while simultaneously seeking enjoyment. The measure of deep relaxation is no longer the amount of time spent at rest but rather how easy and effective it is.

We usually think of sweet desserts as "guilty pleasures" because they give us those two feelings. We feel guilty about a high-calorie intake that still leaves us satisfied enough to throw our cares away. People want to be free from such guilty feelings. We crave a healthy and yet tasty, effective, and enjoyable diet and fitness routine. *Consumer Trend Insights 2022* dubs this a trend toward "Healthy Pleasures," where one needs to derive pleasure from one's health management. Rather than a philosophy of "No pain, no gain," people are seeking a style of fitness and health management that is enjoyable throughout its process and in its results. How did health management, which used to be rigorous and painful, become so hip and trendy? Let's take a closer look at the health management routines of the devotees of Healthy Pleasures.

Fun and Sustainable Healthy Pleasures

The younger generations are showing a keen interest in staying healthy. They may skip a meal, but they never miss taking their seven or eight types of daily health supplements. For instance, a certain German vitamin supplement sold out at its local launch, despite costing 5,000 won per daily dose. Modern people take numerous health supplements such as vitamins, probiotics, and collagen, as if they were taking out an insurance. As exhaustion piles on, so has the demand for products that can provide perfect relaxation, ranging from lightweight and mini electric massagers to premium mattresses. And more people are seeking ways to take care of their mental health as well, through meditation or psycho-therapy, in addition to managing their physical well-being. What is the reason behind the younger generation's interest in their health?

We're not just remarking on a quantitative change in young people's interest. We should note that the perception of health among those in their 20s and 30s is quite different from that of older generations. Good health used to mean the absence of aches and pains. These days health and fitness is not a question of whether you are afflicted with a disease but rather how satisfied you feel about your state of health or well-being. This is why people want to gauge their physical health, find a solution that is best suited to them, and then revel in the satisfaction of having good health. In other words, health and fitness is the epitome of self-management.

Such changes prove we are now living in an age where health and fitness trumps all. This is a highly health-centric perspective that supersedes materialism. The Healthy Pleasure trend has emerged as a "human upgrade업글인간" strategy for this health-centric era. Fitness routines that used to be laborious, difficult, and rigorous are changing to ones that are more easily manageable, enjoyable, and feasible. It's not a health regimen for the older generations pursuing a longer life span, but a more sustainable fitness routine for people of today who are seeking to find happiness in their true selves. To them, maintaining one's health is a fun activity.

There are three notable Healthy Pleasure methods. The first is a dietary regimen in which one seeks healthy yet tasty meals. The second focuses on managing fatigue. For modern people, time for relaxation and sleep are becoming increasingly atypical, and focused methods for relaxation are squeezed into their schedules whenever possible. Finally, there is the need to take care of one's mental health, in which consolation and enjoyment are sought amid a constant stream of anxiety. Let's take a closer look at how people of today are pursuing their Healthy Pleasures.

1. Dietary regimen: Must be healthy and tasty

"I think it's better not to stress out and give up than it is to go through an arduous process only to quit. Let's begin a dietary regimen together. If we are going to diet, we might as well enjoy it!"

This is a post from an online community website, commenting on the pain of being constantly on a diet. It ends with a new Korean slang word, an acronym, "어·다·행·다 어차피 다이어트할 거 행복하게 다이어트한다" meaning "If we are going to diet, we might as well enjoy it." A strict dietary regimen is difficult to maintain and is often short-lived. Recently there has been a boom in the health community among those seeking a "happier diet" which seeks both healthy and tasty meals. Rather than limiting one's menu to chicken breasts and sweet potatoes, which often symbolize a dietary regimen, these Healthy Pleasure enthusiasts seek out substitutes ranging from the healthier versions of "junk food" or low-calorie dishes that are covered in exciting and so-called "worldly flavors" such as konjac *tteok-bokki*떡볶이 and chicken breast dumplings to desserts such as chocolate-flavored protein brownies and sugar-free strawberry-flavored ice cream.

Whoever said "good medicine tastes bitter?" Among the myriad of photos on Instagram with the hashtag #healthy-meal#건강식단, we rarely find dishes that we usually equate with a healthy diet containing vegetables and low sodium. In fact, we would not even be able to recognize it as such without the hashtag since most are bright and colorful and resemble ordinary tasty-looking dishes. Grilled chicken breast with a side of diced chilly-peppers and mustard sauce – a healthier version of the infamous stringy spring onion found on fried chicken – as well as sweet and sour spicy noodles that substitute semi-dried tofu for the noodles, and tasty spaghetti aglio e olio, are but some of the dishes that feature in the posts as taste becomes just as important as calorie content.

The numbers speak for themselves. According to Konan Technology's analysis of responses to healthy meals, "healthy" was linked more to terms like "unappetizing" prior to October 2020. And since then, health and dietary dishes often evoke terms such as "tasty" and "healthy" together, indicating a recent and notably solid emphasis on taste regarding healthy food.

The younger age groups in their 20s and 30s have also emerged as a key consumer demographic in the health supplements market since the outbreak of COVID-19. Where the younger generations of the past were more focused on supplements that helped suppress their appetites to cut down on caloric intake, using them as a tool to enhance their looks, recently they have widened their interest and scope of products. According to the Korea Health Supplements Association, purchases of health supplements by those in their 20s and 30s each jumped by 47.9 percent and 56.8 percent, respectively, in 2020 from a year earlier. Accordingly, online shopping platforms more popular among the younger generations such as Musinsa무신사, Olive Young올리브영 and Market Kurly마켓컬리, have increased their range of health supplements on offer. Musinsa, which targets male consumers in their 20s and 30s, began featuring more than 170 "inner beauty" products and health supplements from April 2021.

And the health supplements market has also evolved in line with a younger pool of consumers. Products that placed emphasis on their effects and properties are now beginning to focus on their taste and texture. Drugmakers and supplements manufacturers have started to roll out a wider range of products in different forms and flavors, such as jellies, gummies, juices, and dissolving strips. Smaller companies are trying to appeal to their newer clients with unique flavors and eye-catching designs and packaging. For example, a company unveiled a product that mixed honey with cultivated ginseng, called the "Ginseng Honey Jar산양삼 꿀단지," and another launched an edible collagen in fig flavor무화과 콜라겐 that appealed to a younger audience with its unique taste and easy-to-open packaging. There is also a boxed package of different apple-flavored supplements called "Your Body My Body Gummy Vitamins너뭄내뭄 비타민젤리" that won awards for its colorful design and branding. Protein supplements, which were only available in powder form and were exclusive to health fanatics and bodybuilders, began to appear as health drinks, energy bars, and brownies, drawing a wider pool of consumers. Maeil Dairies, a trailblazer in the local dairy market, launched a protein drink called "Celex" in October 2018, initially targeting elderly customers. However, as younger customers began snapping up the drinks, the company began to adjust the flavors. It racked up 90 billion won ($76 million) in revenue after its release of a peach-flavored protein drink product in March 2021 that targeted a younger female demographic.

And along with the trend for delicious healthy meals, a preference for vegan diets has also emerged. We should note that afficionados of Healthy Pleasures do not adhere to a strict vegan regimen three times a day, seven days a week. They empathize with vegan values and choose to include vegan options in their dietary regime once or twice a week, deriving a sense of accomplishment from their "selective vegan lifestyle." Vegan bistros and restaurants that offer mouth-watering fare as well as a chic atmosphere are making inroads in the hip Gangnam, Hongdae, and Itaewon areas. Some foodies have begun to share online lists of top vegan eateries that feature dishes that can even appeal to non-vegans. Vegan dishes are not limited to salads full of vegetables. Renowned vegan diners feature coconut curries, or burgers made with black soybean patties infused with the aroma of a charcoal grill. And even amid social distancing restrictions, people clamor to be on the waiting list for a reservation at these popular diners.

2. Fatigue management: Must be healthy and efficient

Modern people yearn for complete relaxation but are often unable to achieve it. One of the biggest dilemmas for the younger generations in their 20s and 30s is how to relax efficiently. In the humdrum of modern society, there is only a limited amount of time allowed for relaxation. Adherents of Healthy Pleasures seek to strategize a more efficient solution that best fits their personal needs. For instance, an increasing number of people are on the prowl for the perfect pillow that affords them quality sleep in a limited time. These so-called "pillow nomads" go through countless pillows in their grave search for "The One" that perfectly suits them. After careful consideration of the height, cushioning, and angle of numerous pillows, when they find "The One" they yell "Eureka!" and put an end to their nomadic wanderings.

Amid a rising number of insomniacs among those in their 20s and 30s due to a lack of time, sleep deprivation, or continuous fatigue regardless of the amount of time spent in bed, the market dedicated to enhancing the quality of sleep has grown by leaps and bounds. Such determination on the part of the younger generations, and their willingness to invest unlimited resources into achieving a good night's rest, has given rise to the neologism "sleeponomics슬리포노믹스." And as couples had to forgo luxurious honeymoons to exotic locations, a large portion of their expenses were diverted to setting up the interiors of their new homes. Coupled with sleeponomics, this drove up the premium on bedroom furnishings such as mattresses, bedframes, and bedding. The number of consumers spending more than 10 million won on such exorbitant furnishings between January and April of 2021 more than doubled from the same period a year earlier.

Along with the quantitative growth of the sleep-related market came the enhanced quality of the industry. As demand for quality and effective sleep rose among those in their 20s and 30s, a rising number of consumers are searching for their own unique sleeping solutions through various sleep-related content. These insomniacs utilize smartwatch apps such as "AutoSleep," "Pillow," and "Sleep Cycle" to determine their sleep patterns. The apps are finding a following among a younger crowd as they allow them to gauge their sleep duration, sleep cycles, how much they tossed and turned, and whether they snored or talked in their sleep. Social media content with titles such as "10-minute stretches that induce a good night's sleep" and "Tips for a sound sleep" have a considerable following. YouTube searches on "sleep" yield an array of related content, ranging from "sleep-inducing music that knocks you out in 10 minutes" to "the four-and-a-half-hour guide to sleep management." Videos that contain ASMRs of white noise, or brainwave sounds that promise immediate sleep, all boast high view counts.

3. Mental health: Must be healthy and enjoyable

The last form of Healthy Pleasure is taking care of one's emotional well-being. People want to take care of their mental health but find counseling too taxing. They want to relieve their anxiety but find it difficult to unburden all their stories. The quickest and easiest solution is searching their daily fortunes or horoscopes that offer a wide range of predictions, from outlooks for their relationships to wealth and employment. It's a minor "healing method" to attain some lightweight advice and consolation, rather than more serious predictions that may tip the scales. Social media has seen a rising number of posts on daily fortunes and horoscopes. Their hashtags yield more than 110,000 and 140,000 posts, respectively (as of August 2021). YouTube has an array of channels related to tarot card readings such as 'Tarot Horang타로호랑' and 'Tarot Myomyo타로묘묘', and videos of their readings are gaining quite the following. The tarot reader will pick groups of one to five random cards, assigning a number to each group. The viewer then chooses a number, and the reading or interpretation of those cards begin. The tarot reader's fee comes in the form of "likes" and "subscriptions" from viewers. Comments on these videos are another form of play and "mental healing" as viewers share how accurately (or not) their fortunes came true.

Such phenomena are not limited to South Korea alone. Anxiety over the future has prompted a surge in demand for horoscopes and astrology, especially among young people. According to Google Trends, searches for "birth chart" and "astrology" each hit five-year highs in 2020 due to rising anxiety prompted by the viral outbreak, according to a BBC report. This in turn fueled a growth in related apps such as "Co-Star" and "Sanctuary."

As more people were forced to stay indoors during the pandemic, finding a solution for listlessness and lethargy also emerged as a demanding task in mental healthcare. Tik-

Tok users have been uploading challenges aimed at shaking off feelings of lethargy and burn-out#무기력극복챌린지. These videos show TikTokers challenging themselves in month-long endeavors to focus on certain projects or activities to pull themselves out of a rut. Most of these 30-day challenges are surprisingly run-of-the-mill affairs, such as taking pictures of the sky, filing their nails, binging on live performance videos of their "bias," or favorite members of a group. They may seem trivial, so much so that it's hard to imagine that these tasks would offer a sense of accomplishment. But the main point is that these "challenges" are not that difficult. They're activities so easy that one feels compelled to complete them. Those that undertake them share their progress and leave evidence of their accomplishments, finding solace among others who are on a similar track. The reason for their popularity is that such mundane challenges allow people to find their own happiness by racking up small accomplishments of their own.

Startling changes in views on psychotherapy are also welcome. Counseling and psychotherapy in general were considered taboo in South Korea, due to a lack of proper public awareness, unlike other advanced nations such as the U.S. or in Europe. Changes are afoot in the local scene as many have come to accept lighter and more approachable forms of therapy through art, children's fables, or yoga. Online educational platform CLASS101's course on "Soul Searching through Art with a Certified Art Therapist" involves drawing or painting pictures and learning about oneself. The last session of the course allows students to put together all their artwork in the form of their very own "art journal." Another course titled "The Secret Fable Room for Grownups" allows attendees to make their own interpretations of famous folk tales and learn about their own thoughts and emotions. Sharing a variety of interpretations of the same story in the form of comments allows people to come to listen to different viewpoints and reach their own conclusions and understanding. Such online therapy courses are finding a following among those in their 20s and 30s as they are not restricted by time or space and provide attendees with a level of enjoyment and consolation. Such changes have led to the registration of around 400 private licenses related to counseling in 2021.

Background: Health Is on Everyone's Minds

Health has been an important subject for thousands of years and will always continue to be of central interest for humanity. And yet the paradigm for health management, one of the most basic of human instincts, is shifting smoothly from one of "perseverance and restraint" to one of "enjoyment and comfort." Let's take a look at the reason behind this novel change and why it has become so important to the younger generations.

1. COVID-19: Importance of health hits home

The pandemic obviously served as the ultimate trigger for everyone's focus on health. The viral outbreak brought with it a fear of infection as well as a realization of the value of one's health. The novel influenza known as H1N1 in 2009 and the MERS (Middle East respiratory syndrome) outbreak in 2015 also triggered a similar focus on health. Figures at the time prove as much: sales of health supplements surged immediately following both epidemics. According to global data analytics and brand consulting firm Kantar Group, sales of red ginseng products jumped 57 percent following the spread of H1N1 in July 2009, while those of vitamins and other health supplements rose by 15 percent after the MERS outbreak in June 2015. The ongoing pandemic also prompted a keen interest in health. A survey of 1,000 adult men and women in May 2021 conducted by the Korea Chamber of Commerce and Industry showed that 78.1 percent of respondents have a heightened interest in their health.

This is not just limited to physical health. The two-year pandemic has forcibly cut off social interaction and pushed some people to the brink of a nervous breakdown. The collapse of daily routines and the ensuing spread of depression gave rise to the term "corona blues." According to the Ministry of Health and Welfare's comprehensive review of the general population affected by mental health issues due to COVID-19 in the first quarter of 2021, 22.5 percent of people surveyed were diagnosed as at risk for depression, six times the level of 2018. This has naturally led to physical and mental health issues emerging as the hottest topic of interest during this period.

2. Every man for himself:
Health becomes a survival strategy

Chalking up the Healthy Pleasures trend's rise merely to the viral outbreak does not do it justice. As we previously outlined, Korean society has become increasingly segmented, ultimately resulting in a Nano Society. Communities have scattered and every person has become an island, not knowing the identity of the person next to them. This has prompted people to try and survive in a world where it's "every man for himself," where they can only trust in themselves. It has become only natural to take care of one's own health. In a Nano Society, faith in each other quickly disintegrates while anxiety grows. Anxiety is one of the most basic of human emotions. From the standpoint of evolutionary psychology, anxiety is essential to human survival. Anxiety drives people to avoid danger and proactively protect themselves. The anxiety that currently pervades society has also prompted people to take protective measures, most notably in the form of buying health supplements and working out. Experts point out that people have been expressing their economic and political anxieties in the form of investing in their health over the past few years.

3. Changes in attitudes of millennials and Gen Zers toward health

We should note, in particular, the changes in the attitudes of millennials and Gen Zers toward looking after one's health. Open Survey, a firm specializing in mobile research, questioned 1,000 adult men and women on what a healthy life means to them. One 25-year-old woman replied that it means working out three times a week, having a drink once in a while, regularly meeting up with friends, and enjoying hobbies or leisure during the weekend. As such views indicate, the younger generations want to be healthy and at the same time aren't willing to miss out on the joys of life. Taking care of their health is another form of loving themselves. Such changes in the perception of health and fitness among the younger generations has provided a wider base for the Healthy Pleasures trend in everyday life.

Healthy Pleasures are not just about drinking chocolate-flavored protein beverages or poring through the daily horoscope to try and shake off one's anxieties. We see a more serious approach as well, most notably through YouTube videos uploaded by young people suffering from cancer or rare terminal illnesses that serve as their personal "treatment vlogs." They sip from a mug of coffee as they go through chemotherapy, show their trivial daily routines such as having a steak dinner, and reach out and communicate with their unknown viewers. They want to send a message that living with a disease does not mean that they're always sad or lack vigor. They show themselves drawing up bucket lists even as they receive treatment, striking a rapport with viewers who sent them messages of support. Healthy Pleasures may provide some people with a way of loving themselves and enjoying their daily happiness, and to others a reason for living beyond a simple lifestyle.

Outlook and Implications

— From medical treatment to preventative medicine: "Early Care Syndrome"

Healthy Pleasures can be construed as the first step of our society's transition from medical treatment toward preventative medicine. The market needs to take note of "Early Care Syndrome" among the younger generations more familiar with preemptive measures. "Early Care Syndrome" refers to the young strata of society taking preventative measures to mitigate various health-related issues that may occur later in life. One notable example is hair loss management routines. Such concerns which were more prevalent among those in their 40s or older, have become a "preventative" issue for those in their 20s and 30s. Such views are evident in revenues from anti-hair loss shampoo, with their target consumers expanding from those in their 40s and 50s to the younger demographics. CJ Olive Young reported that sales of products related to hair loss treatment have jumped by 40 percent each year, with the largest growth among women in their 20s.

The largest increase among patients seeking treatment for high blood pressure in the past five years were of those in their 20s. Such is their determination to proactively detect and curtail potential health issues seen among the older generations. This will likely become even more severe as people gain easier access to health-related data and information in a digitized society. As people's "healthy life" expectancy shortens despite a longer life span, the younger generation are increasingly exhibiting signs of "Early Care Syndrome," hoping to sustain a healthy and happy life in a modern society.

Fitness needs to be hip: The search for "Fitness +α"

The most notable implication of the Healthy Pleasure trend is that "health and fitness need to be trendy." Fitness for adherents of Healthy Pleasures is never outdated or mundane. It is fresh, hip, and becomes more enjoyable the more it is pursued. As such, companies need to keep close tabs on what consumers seek for their "plus alpha $(+\alpha)$" factor – that added "something" that will help them more enjoyably manage their health.

First off, makers of health supplements, arguably some of the biggest earners during the pandemic, need to diversify their strategies to hold onto their new clients, namely those in their 20s and 30s. They need to design "custom-tailored" health products to meet their needs or provide a unique consumer experience to target the younger demographic. "Personalized" health foods are also making rapid inroads into the market.

Manufacturers of bedroom furnishings and other sleep-related products are expected to infuse a "technological" aspect to appeal to their younger targets. In fact, "sleep tech" has been a buzzword in recent years at the Consumer Electronics Show (CES) held annually in Las Vegas. The use of sleep tech to manage one's "sleep care," will eventually evolve into a "sleep cure." If sleep care provided for the needs of the consumer, a sleep cure will hopefully step up to provide a solution for the problems facing consumers, such as providing an effective treatment for insomnia.

Counseling and therapy will also likely expand its reach. Social taboos and barriers will likely fade away as the public finds fun and enjoyable ways to approach therapy. According to a survey conducted by the UnivTomorrow Research

Laboratory대학내일 20대연구소, seven out of ten millennials and Gen Zers replied that they need ways to manage their stress and mental health. Those who sought professional help stood at a mere 6.4 percent. Still, a whopping 74.2 percent replied they wanted to seek help from a therapist or expert, showing a clear interest in mental healthcare. With the rising frequency of personal counseling, the local market shows signs of expanding in the near future.

Healthcare, which had previously been a mundane affair, is rapidly transforming in line with social changes in society, between generations and in keeping with the times. Healthy Pleasures go beyond South Korea as a trend in 2022, signaling a changing paradigm for healthcare in general. The market must respond to the demand for more sustainable approaches to health management by meeting the consumer demand that "health management should be fun, too!"

Opening the X-Files on the 'X-teen' Generation

While local media has recently been focusing on millennials and Gen Zers born during the 1980s and 1990s, those who still command the consumer market, both in the quantitative and qualitative senses, are members of Generation X – those born between 1965 and 1979. We would like to zero in on the core group, the so-called "Gen X-teens엑스틴," who were born during the 1970s. These Gen X-teens (1) spent their formative years in a relatively prosperous period, both culturally and economically, that helped form a freethinking and individualistic mindset, which has allowed them to (2) share a lifestyle with their teenage children. At a time when society was going through a historical period of digital transformation, these X-teens were vanguards of major social, economic, political, and cultural changes during a tumultuous era of transition from a dictatorship to a fully democratic society.

Gen X-teens have become a major consumer force as they now enter their forties. As they mature into adulthood as members of the "Money-friendly Generation," they have emerged as the movers and shakers among consumers of the e-commerce industry, helping lay the foundation for this innovative service in the market. Still, they are the quintessential "sandwiched generation," stuck between the conflict of the older generations and of millennials and Gen Zers. Nevertheless, X-teens form the backbone of our society. They take on the roles of veteran players as well as coaches, forming the core of an organization, and are a leading consumer power in the market. Companies should win the hearts of these Gen X-teens if they are to dominate the market as X-teens will remain the leading consumers in the Korean market for quite some time.

The 2020 Tokyo Olympics, belatedly held in 2021, highlighted the outstanding talents of Gen Zers. Their composure and strength in the face of adversity and failure, remaining unfazed by the stream of online abuse, changed public perceptions of the Games and Olympians. After teen table tennis sensation Shin Yu-bin bowed out in the third round of the women's singles, she uploaded a post on social media thanking her fans for their words of encouragement which gave her strength, adding, "I was a tad disappointed, but I will soon shrug it off." The public's infatuation with only gold medalists in the past, which left silver medalists to hang their heads in shame, is no more. And such changes are not just limited to the players. Gen Z fans are showing quite a different attitude when watching the Games compared with the older generations. They were more interested in seeing the players do their best until the very end and face their results with pride. They were vocal in their appreciation for players, even ones on the opposing teams, who displayed outstanding manners and sportsmanship. Koo Jeong-woo, Professor of Sociology at Sungkyunkwan University in

Seoul, noted that Olympic spectators' focus has shifted from the successes and failures of Olympians as representatives of their nation to the endeavors and effort of each individual player.

In fact, this is not the first generation to focus on "the individual" rather than "the organization." Before Generation Z born in the 1990s, Generation X born in the 1970s ushered in an era of individualism. Truth be told, Gen Xers have been brushed aside as obsolete by a fresh discourse over millennials and Gen Zers. The spotlight has somewhat shifted to those born in the 1980s and 1990s as they emerge as the leading consumers. It may seem par for the course as the younger generations absorb new services and keep apace with rapid changes in society. Here we should note that these Gen Zers were raised by Gen Xers.

The term "Generation X" signifies the unknown factor, stemming from a book of the same name penned during the 1960s based on a collection of interviews with the "mysterious" teenagers of that decade. The letter 'x' is often used in algebra to indicate a value that is yet unknown. And as 'y' follows 'x' in the alphabet, the youths that immediately followed were called "Generation Y," more commonly referred to as "millennials" since they ushered in the third millennium. Their successor in turn, going down the alphabet, were dubbed "Generation Z," or "Gen Zers." As outlined, Generation X was the first to headline a discourse on youths.

Their emergence at the time was shocking, much more so than that of millennials and Gen Zers. Popular media was at a loss as to how to accept them, and they took center stage in most controversial issues at the time. When referring to Generations X, Y, Z, or those who preceded them and those that will follow, members' birth years differ according to various scholars; but if we are to define each in terms more commonly used in popular media, it would look similar to the following table.

Name		Year of Birth	Age in 2022	Nicknames
Older Generations	Industrial Generation	Prior to 1954	68 and older	*Saemaul* Generation
	Baby Boomers	1955-1964	58-67	Cornerstone Generation, Bohemians
Generation X	Older Generation X	1965-1969	53-57	Seo Taiji Generation '88 Olympic Generation
	Younger Generation X	1970-1979	43-52	X-teens, Beeper or Cellphone Generation
Millennials, Gen Z	Millennials	1980-1994	28-42	*Infinite Challenge Generation* '02 World Cup Generation
	Generation Z	1995-2009	13-27	Livestream Generation YouTube Generation
Generation α		2010 and up	12 and younger	TikTok Generation

Now we will take a closer look at Generation X, especially the group that *Consumer Trend Insights* would like to dub "X-teens," – that is, the Gen Xers who are similar to teenagers in the sense that they share a similar lifestyle with their teenage children. These X-teens like to upload clips on TikTok with their children, assuming the role of a "frienddy프렌디 (friend+daddy)." We will open the X-files on the formerly unquantifiable Generation X to explore their ideals and realities, as well as their achievements and frustrations.

Where Have All the Gen Xers Gone?

In June 2021, the political scene was stunned when a rookie 36-year-old took the helm of the nation's largest opposition party. It was the first time in history for anyone in their thirties to chair a major political party. Of course, party chairs are not assumed according to age. But it was a sensation for a millennial, without any experience as a lawmaker, to take the top position of a conservative party, or any political party for that matter. The corporate sector has also been focusing on millennials and Gen Zers. The title of "youngest ever" executive or outside director of the board usually goes to those born in the 1980s. So, here emerges a question: Where are the Gen Xers in their forties and fifties who form the backbone of any organization? We often hear the grumblings of Gen Xers who have to take cues and walk on eggshells dealing with their juniors born in the 1990s. They are no longer of interest in popular media which is more wrapped up in the slew of reports on millennials and Gen Zers, and we hardly see any articles about the present-day challenges faced by Gen Xers, the movers and shakers of the 1990s. Gone are the days when those born in the 1970s were the hottest issue. So where have all the Gen Xers gone?

Defining 'Generation X' and 'X-teens'

"Generation X" refers to those born in the 1970s who spent their formative teenage years during the 1990s. *Consumer Trend Insights 2022* would like to shed light on the "X-teens" in particular – that is, those born between 1970 and 1979 who (1) spent their formative years in a relatively prosperous period, both culturally and economically, that helped form a freethinking and individualistic mindset, which has allowed them to (2) share a lifestyle with their teenage Generation Z and α children. And because marriage and childrearing have evolved in an atypical manner, we cannot define all Gen Xers as X-teens. Even among Gen Xers, there are various types of families, including those who prefer to remain single, single parents, those whose children are still toddlers, and couples who prefer to be DINKs, or "double-income, no kids." The most common type of X-teen is a Gen Xer born during the 1970s whose cultural and social upbringing during their teens had an impact on their consumer patterns. In other words, these are people in their forties who possess a teenage lifestyle and mindset.

Gen Xers witnessed dizzying advances in the 1980s and 1990s. Their teenage experiences that informed their values and cultural codes in particular became the basis for their current consumer culture. As such, we should trace back their formative years before dissecting their current lifestyle.

Let's take those born in 1975 as a median group. The 1980s and 1990s they experienced was a time of upheaval in terms of the nation's culture, economy, politics, and society. Those born that year were just 12 at the time of the June Democratic Uprising of 1987. They were attending public schools국민학교 (*gukmin hakgyo*), which were considered remnants of the Japanese colonial era, rather than the elementary schools초등학교 (*chodeung hakgyo*) of today, at the time when Seoul hosted the Summer Olympic Games in 1988 and when the South Korean government finally allowed outbound travel for all citizens. The 1980s also saw the nation show its potential as an economic powerhouse amid brisk exports and as positive results of rapid industrialization began to show. Rather than urging people to scrimp and save, they were encouraged to enjoy the fruits of their labor and spend money on luxuries such as cars, refrigerators, and hi-fi stereos. Gen Xers were the first generation to learn how to freely express themselves and focus on what gave them joy.

Seo Taiji, JY Park, Bang Si-hyuck, Na Young-seok, Kim Tae-ho, Yoo Jae-suk…

The current movers and shakers of the media industry are all Gen Xers. And this is no coincidence. They all spent their formative years during the 1990s when the nation went through major turning points, and they were the first to experience the aftermaths. The debut of Seo Taiji and Boys in 1992 in particular was culturally symbolic. Teenagers at the time talked about its members, listened to their music, and emulated their fashion. Their appearance hailed a shakeup in the music industry, shifting more toward teens. Gen Xers were the first to begin fandoms and were the first to "geek out덕질" over their so-called "idols."

They were also the first generation to embrace new technology such as personal computers and "beepers," or pagers. The hugely popular tvN drama *Reply 1988*응답하라 1988, in which the late 1980s and early 1990s served as the backdrop, depicts a main character holding impromptu quizzes in a HiTEL chatroom, one of Korea's first bulletin board systems (BBS), with his landline modem-linked PC. In fact, PCs and beepers were widely used as tools for amusement and socializing. When these Gen Xers began their first jobs, the nation had made the transition to high-speed internet. The introduction of iPhones and KakaoTalk during their thirties ushered in an era of mobile communication. In other words, Gen Xers were first to live through all phases of the digital era, from PC, to online, and to mobile communications. They were in the eye of the storm, experiencing firsthand the beginnings and ends of major turning points in Korea's modernizing society, including the nation's development to a full democracy, its baby steps in the consumer market, the transition from analog to digital, and the explosion of pop culture.

Refocusing on X-teens

So, why should we now bring X-teens back into the spotlight? Well, we should note that X-teens constitute a sizeable stratum of the population and are major spenders in the market. According to a July 2021 report by the Ministry of the Interior and Safety on demographic statistics of registered residents, people in their forties were the second most populous age group at 15.9 percent, closely behind those in their fifties at 16.6 percent. If we expand the scope of Generation X to those in their forties and fifties, their combined 32.5 percent outweighs any other generational group, with those in their twenties and thirties at 26.2 percent and those in their sixties and seventies at 20.7 percent. Gen Xers are also the biggest consumers. In terms of life stages, many of them are in their child-rearing phase, with their kids attending middle and high schools. They are at the apex of their spending cycle in terms of living and educational expenses, and in terms of their intentions to seek larger housing.

According to Statics Korea's 2020 household spending report, monthly average spending by heads of households under the age of 39 stood at 2.38 million won ($2000), those between 40 and 49 at 3.09 million won ($2600), those between 50 and 59 at 2.78 million won ($2350), and those 60 and above at 1.7 million won ($1430). If millennials are the first generation in Korea's history to be less affluent than their parents, those in their forties and fifties are conversely the first to fare better than their parents and their children.

The X-teen impact on consumption is also noteworthy. Millennials and Gen Zers may be early adopters of new products and services, but Gen Xers are the ones who allow them to establish themselves in the market. In her 2021 book *The Young Forties: The Return of Generation X*, author Sun Mi Lee focuses on the "Young Forties영포티" who share common consumer traits with millennials. Both groups shop online and offline, keep up to date with the latest trends, and are open to new technology and services. However, as these Young Forties have greater spending power than millennials, brands that fail to coax them to open their wallets inevitably fail in expanding their market share.

Generation X, who triggered the heated discourse on generations, have become the backbone of society and are now considered part of the older generations. So, how does the market in which they participate differ from that of their progenitors, the baby boomers? We will take a closer look at the changes brought on by their distinctive consumer patterns and their implications for 2022.

The Lifestyles of X-teens

1. The generation that thinks outside the box

In July 1994, two women wearing crop tops stood trial on minor misdemeanor charges. It may be difficult to imagine now, but there was a time when fashion that excessively exposed the skin led to arrests. To the older generations, the stylings of Generation X were disconcerting enough to warrant legal action.

X-teens who challenged social taboos and conventions of the older generations, with their battle cry of "my own individuality," are still defying social norms in their forties. To start off, "genderless" spending, which breaks boundaries between the sexes, is a major keyword. If the so-called OPAL (old people with active lives) generation are still mired by conventions according to age and gender in their spending, X-teens are similar to millennials and Gen Zers in that they are not bound by the gender divide. The beauty industry is one such sector. Middle-aged men in their forties are a rapidly emerging consumer group for beauty and skincare brands. Online shopping platform 11Street saw a 132 percent jump in sales of beauty products among customers in their forties during the first half of 2020, with an emphasis on "functional cosmetics" that aim to brighten the skin and ward off facial wrinkles. In other words, men in their forties are not only interested in skincare but are now more pro-actively taking care of their appearance. As such, cosmetics companies are releasing products exclusive for men in line with these changes.

X-teens were also the first generation to become "fan-boys" and "fangirls" that actively "geeked out" over their favorite idols. After Seo Taiji and Boys burst onto the music scene, the 1st generation idol group H.O.T. gave rise to a massive female fandom known as "*Oppa* Troops오빠부대," with their deafening screams of "*oppa!*" – the honorific term for one's older brother, male acquaintance, or even boyfriend. These passionate fans would save up their pocket money to buy cassette tapes, posters, photos, and concert tickets of their favorite idol groups. Fast forward to the 21st century where another group has emerged to help revitalize the now forty-something X-teens' "geek out" days: BTS. It would be unfair to assume that a parent would naturally be interested in idol groups that their middle and high-school children rave about. Rather, X-teen fandoms of current idol groups are of their own making, separate from that of their children. There is no conclusive data, but industry experts believe that there are a considerable number of fans in their forties and fifties among the BTS fandom known as "ARMY."

There are numerous posts on online support communities for mothers, known as "mom cafés," that claim they live for Tuesdays because that's when the global band uploads new episodes of *Run BTS!*달려라 방탄, their own variety show, on Naver's V LIVE online channel, as well as on its fandom platform Weverse under its HYBE label.

The impact of X-teens' "geek outs," armed with considerable spending power, is more substantial than one can imagine. In October 2020, ARMY members in their forties were among the first in line for stock subscriptions of Big Hit Entertainment's (now HYBE) IPO, the managing company of BTS. To them, buying Big Hit's shares was like collecting BTS merchandise. Some even proudly stated in online posts that their purchases were based on their confidence as long-time fans of Korea's entertainment industry. It's as though X-teens' training since they were teenagers has culminated in this investment moment – the ultimate expression of their fandom culture.

2. Becoming an adult of the "Money-friendly Generation"

The 1990s, when X-teens were teens and young adults, was a period of unprecedented economic growth in South Korea. The nation saw continued growth in real income from the 1980s to the 2010s, as well as growth in spending. Consumers expanded their expenditure from necessities to luxuries. X-teens saw a shift in values from frugal spending and saving to enjoying the fruits of their labor. It gave birth to the original "Money-friendly Generation" who were not afraid of expressing their desires and their individuality through brands and purchases.

These kids of the "Money-friendly Generation" have now become adults. As they enter their forties, there has been a marked shift in the consumer market. If their predecessors, the baby boomers, focused more on spending for their families, X-teens never exclude themselves from the equation. Personal spending is especially evident in self-management and growth. While they maintain a degree of economic stability, X-teens have a propensity for "human upgrades업글인간," unwilling to settle for the status quo. And unlike baby boomers, they were the first generation to see a surge in admittances to colleges and universities. Rather than just identifying themselves as someone's father or mother, they aspire to improve themselves.

Their desire for self-improvement shows in their spending patterns. According to a report on credit card spending by Big Data Consulting, Shinhan Card's consumer pattern analysis think tank, X-teens' expenditure at bookstores and on online classes had increased during the first half of 2021 from the same period in 2019. Five local online educational platforms, including CLASS101클래스101 and mobile-based Mybiskit마이비스킷, saw a decline of 16.1 percent in the proportion of female users in their twenties over a two-year period, while that of women in their forties rose 7.9 percent over the same period. Purchases of online home physical training sessions also saw their biggest increase among customers in their forties. The proportion of credit card charges for online fitness training sessions by those in their twenties dipped to 27 percent in the first half of 2021, compared with 43 percent two years earlier. On the other hand, the same expenditure among customers in their forties rose by seven percentage points to 21 percent in the same period.

X-teens were also behind the spectacular rise of the e-commerce market following the outbreak of COVID-19, as they were able to quickly adapt to making online purchases based on their experience with the previous transition from analog to digital. According to the Ministry of Science and ICT's annual report on internet usage, 86.3 percent of people in their forties logged on to online shopping platforms in 2020, up 15 percentage points from the previous year. According to a report titled "Changes in Generational Spending Patterns and its Implications" by Hana Institute of Finance, the think tank arm of Hana Bank, online credit card charges among those in their forties and older jumped 49 percent in 2020 from the previous year. Spending on e-commerce platforms, including Coupang쿠팡 and Gmarket G마켓 in particular, showed a growth rate 1.8 times higher among fortysomethings than that of thirtysomethings and younger. X-teens, who became familiar with the internet as teenagers, have emerged as big spenders in online markets.

Retailers are releasing mobile apps tailored toward these new fortysomething customers. If many customers in their forties previously believed that clothing should only be bought after trying them on at offline stores, X-teens enjoy browsing and shopping for the latest fashion on their mobile phones. ZigZag지그재그, a fashion and shopping app previously exclusive to millennials and Gen Zers, launched its sister platform Posty포스티 in the second half of 2021, with a wide range of brands targeting their more mature customers with thicker wallets. Queenit퀸잇, a leader among local online fashion platforms also tailored to a more mature clientele, saw more than 1.4 million downloads in nine months since its launch in September 2020. Trade on the platform jumped 300 percent every month, proving the potential in fashion platforms that target mothers. Musinsa무신사, a major online shopping platform, which initially saw explosive growth by targeting younger millennials and Gen Zers, is also reportedly planning to launch a service by the end of 2021 geared toward customers in their forties and fifties.

Enticing X-teens who tend to remain loyal to their favored brands has become somewhat of a "cheat code" among insiders in the retail industry. "Cheat codes" usually refer to a series of keyboard or button combinations used by gamers to sneakily advance levels. Millennial and Gen Zers may be the first ones to try new services, but it is X-teens who have the power to lay the foundation of innovative services in the market. They were key to the meteoric success of Market Kurly마켓컬리, which has managed to become a giant that threatens more established online retailers in just six years since its 2015 launch. According to a report on overnight mobile orders of fresh produce and food deliveries in June 2021 released by industry tracker WiseApp, customers in their forties and fifties make up 35.4 percent and 23.1 percent, respectively, with combined shares that exceed half of Market Kurly's total users. As outlined above, X-teens have been largely behind the recent stellar success of products and services in the market. Hyungrok Choi, CEO of BALAAN발란, an online and mobile shopping mall that focuses on luxury brands, had this to say in a September 2021 interview:

"Our initial strategy after launching our business was to target millennials and Gen Zers. But we found that our customers in their forties racked up the most purchases and had the highest repurchase rate, and as such were responsible for the lion's share of our revenue. Their portion has only grown in recent years, and we have accordingly adjusted our target demographic."

3. Staying abreast of the latest Gen Z trends

The term "Generation MZ," used more commonly in Korea, reflects a tendency to group millennials and Gen Zers together. However, there are distinct differences that separate these two generations. One of the key elements to note is their parents. Baby boomers, often represented in Korea by those born in 1958, the Year of the Dog⁵⁸년 개띠, are parents of millennials, while those of Gen Z are mostly members of Generation X who dominated the 1990s. As parents influence initial spending habits of their children, it is essential to analyze patterns in both parents and their kids.

Baby boomers experienced the devastating aftermath of the Korean War and its ensuing poverty, helping raise the nation's economy from the rubble and playing a key role in its breakneck development and industrialization, more commonly referred to as the "Miracle on the Han River." Their priorities were to put blood, sweat, and tears into coming out on top amidst cut-throat competition to win a chance at a better life for themselves and their families. On the other hand, as parents of Gen Zers, X-teens focused on the "self," placing value on their individuality and freely expressing their tastes and preferences. They were deemed the most progressive among all generations in history and have instilled such values in their children. Gen Zers have inherited their parents' free and progressive values, including a pursuit of diversity, a high regard for fairness, a flexible view on life and marriage, and an identity as part of the planet encompassing humanity and the environment.

X-teens are familiar with having fun and even learning

from their children. Those with teenage children may have, for example, slightly altered profile pictures on messaging apps. In fact, many are more enthusiastic about using filters after learning from their children the use of a myriad of photo editing tools to take selfies on apps such as Naver's SNOW스노우 and Instagram. TikTok is full of clips of Gen X parents and their Gen Z children showing off their chemistry. Some of the more trending hashtags are #familytiktok #가족틱톡 and #familytiktokvideo#가족틱톡영상. Many of them show kids and their parents dancing or attempting the latest challenges. The hashtags garnered 71.7 million and 113,000 views, respectively, as of November 2021.

What is also interesting is that X-teens are not averse to playing games with their children to establish rapport. According to a report by the Ministry of Culture, Sports and Tourism and the Korea Creative Content Agency, 73.1 percent of parents in their thirties play online, mobile, or console games with their children, while 65.1 percent of parents in their forties also took part in similar activities. This shows that many parents use games as a positive means of connecting with their children. Such trends were also evident in group interviews on subscription services held at Seoul National University's Consumer Trend Center. When asked about various subscription packages they wished to subscribe to, many X-teens with middle and high school children picked game subscriptions and rental services for game consoles such as the PS5 and Nintendo Switch.

The reason why X-teen parents can strike up a friendship with their Gen Z kids is because they have similar values. Whereas baby boomer parents demand of their millennial children to "work hard and succeed," X-teens don't necessarily require their kids to win top spots. Instead, they tend to provide support for them to explore various possible avenues. Therefore, they don't always emphasize studying and getting good grades. One example is a steady rise in "student CEOs," those who simultaneously attend school and operate an online business under the guidance and support of their X-teen parents. A search for "teenage bosses10대 사장" on YouTube and social media shows enterprising teenagers that have set up shop making use of their skills and abilities. Their wares range widely from handicrafts such as stationery and accessories to clothing that they bought directly from wholesalers. Behind the increase in entrepreneurial activities of Gen Zers is the support of their "cool" Gen X parents. Rather than hounding them to focus on their studies, they actively help provide solutions or give advice on business management.

4. Stuck between the old and the new

X-teens may have grown up in relative prosperity, but their lives were not without adversity. The nation was rocked by a major crisis as they were about to graduate from college and university. In December 1997, South Korea had to seek an official bailout from the International Monetary Fund (IMF). After they somehow managed to land jobs despite a recession and massive corporate layoffs, they were faced with yet another global financial crisis a decade later in 2008. They experienced two major economic crises at a crucial time when they should have been most active in their careers. Gone were their dreams and illusions of a neverendingly pleasant world, which were replaced by cold and harsh realities. These were times when X-teens learned the rules of survival. Their crisis awareness forced on them the possibility that they can face a hostile environment at any given time, instilling a survival instinct to lay low. X-teens naturally began to give priority to securing a stable position by complying with a company's strict vertical hierarchy and thusly receiving recognition from the organization.

X-teens are now a fixture of middle management and are required to bridge differences between those in their fifties and sixties on one end, and their subordinates in their twenties and thirties on the other. However, many millennials are ill at ease with their immediate superiors in their forties, currently about to be promoted, more so than they are with higher ranked directors in their fifties. Millennials and Gen Zers in their late twenties feel, despite the narrower age gap, that X-teen superiors don't really understand them and always demand they defer to the rules of the organization.

On the other hand, superiors in their fifties and sixties are often dissatisfied with the lack of leadership among X-teen underlings and find them frustrating. X-teens often find themselves stuck between the older "386 Generation386 세대," – a generation name coined in the 1990s for the then thirty-somethings (3) who took part in anti-government demonstrations as student activists during the 1980s (8) and were born in the 1960s (6) hence '386', also the then widely used PC model number, and the up-and-coming younger generations. As such, Gen Xers are often called the "sandwiched generation" or the "bread generation식빵 시대," mocking the collective group for being indistinguishable from one another, as if baked in batches from identical molds.

Moreover, they are often called upon to take on the role of player as well as of coach: they are wanted on the field and to take responsibility as managers. Such demands are now commonplace, in both private and public sectors as they reorganize their departments into smaller cells, or "agile" structures that can respond swiftly and flexibly to rapid changes in the market. The rank-and-files have been streamlined from the conventional top-down chain of head manager부장, senior manager차장, manager과장, assistant manager대리, employee사원, to a more horizontal one that designates more ambiguous ranks using mostly English words such as pro프로, manager매니저, team leader책임, coach코치, or consultant컨설턴트. This has only added to the mental and physical strains piled onto X-teens.

X-teens feel that they have been treated unfairly. They came up the ranks learning new technology and acquiring the experience and know-how without anyone showing them the ropes. When X-teens joined the work force, companies and society in general were undergoing a digital and IT transition, relegating their superiors' skills to the dustbin of obsolescence. X-teens were the ones that taught their seniors how to use word processors, presentation programs, and spreadsheet software. As they are more used to learning and creating results by themselves, they are not used to "micromanaging" according to specific manuals. However, their subordinates require detailed manuals and reasonable work instructions from them. Experts sometimes call Gen Xers and their elders the "map generation," and millennials and Gen Zers the "GPS generation," since they require specific instructions in carrying out their tasks.

Reflecting such generational realities, the bestselling titles on self-improvement at bookstores contain the words "Team Leader팀장." *Lessons on Leadership for the Team Leader, Manners of Speech for the Team Leader*, and *Team Leader Revolution*팀장 리더십 수업 · 팀장의 말투 · 팀장혁명 are some of the bestselling titles in the category. This is further evidence of rapid changes in the corporate culture facing X-teens as more millennials and Gen Zers enter the workforce. Their leadership in the 21st century has grown even more important, especially during the pandemic as many were forced to work from home or away from their offices. X-teens also make the effort, continuously checking themselves so as to not become what their subordinates deride as a "*kkondae*꼰대," Korean slang for an out-of-touch boomer. According to a survey by an advertising agency, internet users in their forties browse the term the most, more than those in their fifties. X-teens are the largest age group taking part in the Kkondae Level Test 꼰대레벨 or 꼰대력 테스트 which has been trending online and on mobile apps for the past year or two. They continuously undergo self-diagnosis to prevent themselves from turning into an old boomer.

Outlook and Implications
— Forming the core of Korea and of the consumer market

Every man is a creature of the age in which he lives. Regardless of whether we are aware of it or not, the age we live in forms the basis of our beliefs and values. Generation X was endowed with numerous nicknames, including the "New Generation," the "IT Generation," the "Globalization Generation," the "De-politicized Generation," and the "Culture Generation." The generation once deemed "radical" in the 1990s with their unique and sometimes disconcerting propensity to defy authority, who were at the forefront of social paradigms with their pursuit of individuality and candor, now seem to have less relevance with today's society. Nevertheless, Generation X are still important. According to a Statistics Korea report, the median age for the nation's population stood at 21.4 in 1975. Median age divides a population in half, with one half younger than this age and the other half older. The country's median age has been rapidly rising ever since, climbing to 34.3 in 2005, 37.3 in 2010 and 43.7 in 2020. This means the core group of the nation's population are currently in their forties. So, what should we prepare in advance to anticipate changes in the market brought on by X-teens, who once represented the iconic "New Generation" of the 1990s and are now society's core members?

First, firms must never make the mistake of neglecting X-teens who are now the key consumers in the market. As we previously outlined, companies will find it difficult to establish their brands in the market without meeting the needs of X-teens. They may have lifestyles similar to those of millennials and Gen Zers, but there are subtle differences. Therefore, it is even more vital for companies to conduct a thorough analysis of X-teen consumers and pick up on these differences. For example, X-teens are familiar with both digital technology as well as the analog aspects of society that they grew up with, such as print media. In fact, the retail industry regards them as the last "print generation" that have an affinity for printed advertisements like flyers and brochures. Whereas millennials and Gen Zers are more attuned to advertisement banners on messaging apps such as KakaoTalk and social media, Gen Xers are drawn to both printed and online advertisements.

Theirs is also a generation that craves information, which provides an opportunity for companies to reach out to these customers through informational and content marketing. X-teens always seek to keep up to date with the latest trends. They were the ones to lead trends in the 1990s, but now they feel they are lagging behind as everyday life and earning a living gets in the way. Retailers targeting X-teens may find it helpful to approach them through informative content to expand their customer pool.

Companies also need to take a more segmented approach. The market itself is becoming more segmented, with more emphasis on individual marketing. Obviously, this applies to different generations as well. Some are even skeptical about dividing up generations by periods of 10 to 15 years. The lightning pace of changes in society has narrowed the range of each generation that shares common values and lifestyles.

Management should also pay attention to their X-teen staff. Recent HR management has focused heavily on millennials and Gen Zers, taking for granted, or even neglecting, their core middle managers: the X-teens. In retrospect,

X-teens adapted to the corporate structure and strived to meet the demands of the company to achieve results in order to survive. Rather than simply demanding that they bridge the divide between older and younger generations, companies should heed their concerns and dilemmas regarding leadership and generational conflict.

X-teens, born during the 1970s and designated with the letter that signifies an unknown factor, began as an "unfathomable generation" but are now taking center stage in society once again. They were the first generation to create an unprecedented shift in social paradigms, laying the foundation for values held by popular culture, millennials and Gen Zers who have followed in their steps. X-teens are making a comeback. Generation X is returning as X-teens and will act as the nation's leading consumers for some time. There has been a new focus on X-teens and their roles, as parents of Gen Zers, as middle management, and as consumers with buying power. We are bound to see interesting and unexpected changes in Korean society brought on by these newly middle-aged consumers.

Routinize Yourself

We are witnessing the birth of a "new breed of humans" who seek to lead a life of their own choosing. Employees draw up their daily schedules and abide by them, and students create their own study chatrooms with people they don't necessarily know and post progress updates. Routines are habits or procedures we undertake each day, and we would like to dub those who wish to maintain control over their lives through these routines in the absence of external regulation "routineers."

There are multiple reasons behind the surge in routineers. Shorter working hours, as well as increased freedom in dividing working and private lives due to the global pandemic, have reinforced a need for self-management. In a Nano Society where it is no longer possible to attain significant success, finding one's "self" has become a pursuit of the trivial joys in life. "Routineers" may be regarded as a continuation of our 2020 keyword of "Elevate Yourself업글인간," but differs slightly in that the earlier trend highlighted the effort made to create a better version of oneself in anticipation for tomorrow, whereas priorities for routineers lie in their attitude towards life: "even if my life is nothing but ordinary, I will still make the most of it."

As such, businesses need to adjust their marketing and communications strategies to support their routineer customers and their sincerely pursued daily lives. HR management also needs to ensure the autonomy of their work practices as well as a system of regular assessment based on feedback to encourage the best possible results. The issue here is that of reliability. The trend of routineers is evidence that trust among people has the potential to support structural management, school education, and even parental guidance. Humans instinctively seek to improve themselves, and thus we need to have faith in our basic nature to seek momentum to push ourselves forward when we are stuck in a rut.

As a force of habit, I play a workout video on YouTube. I watch the video, still lying in bed, vowing to myself, "next time, I will follow along," saving it to a "watch later" list. I feel a prick of guilt seeing the list getting longer and longer. Nevertheless, I feel somewhat relieved to find others like me after reading through the various comments.

The above comments may prick at the conscience of many people. Learning about working out has become quite easy. Even if you do not go to famous fitness centers, there are instructors and workout enthusiasts on YouTube who kindly guide you through various exercises. There are plenty of great videos. The problem is carrying the exercises out. When you have the will but fall short of following through, these daily uploads of home physical training sessions can be a burden for most people. However, there is a tip that may help even the weak-willed among us: the comments that bring you a sigh of relief may also serve to push you along to take part in these sessions every day.

We are living in an age where one must design one's own

daily schedule. Those who are used to overnight self-study sessions may have realized how much the level of autonomy has risen throughout society these days. Most students who were required to stay after classes for their "voluntary" self-study periods between 6 and 10 p.m. will say that these sessions were anything but "voluntary." However, with changes in the curriculum, such heavy-handed sessions are no more. Most students these days head home between 3 and 4 p.m. Afterwards, they follow their own schedules, be it at local study rooms or at private learning institutions. Such trends are not limited to schools. Society on the whole has become more familiar with increased autonomy. Teleworking and remote offices spread rapidly amid the protracted pandemic, while corporate culture evolved into one that encouraged "work-from-anywhere," further enhancing the degree of freedom in people's private lives as well as their working environment.

Modern-day people who must set their own schedules rather than follow ones set for them are finding that "weakness of will" is not a problem that they face alone, but one that challenges all of us. With this sudden "freedom" people of today have to will themselves to keep to their schedules. So how do writers, composers, and others with professions who have long been free of fixed routines accomplish their plans and objectives? Ha Jee Hyun, professor of Psychiatry at Konkuk University in Seoul, says that establishing regularity in life is key. Most people believe that an artist's creativity comes from a free lifestyle, but we often find that successful artists keep to regular routines. French writer Bernard Werber has breakfast at his favorite café every day, writes about 10 pages in the morning, and meets up with people for lunch at around 1 p.m. Bestselling Japanese author Haruki Murakami said in an interview that he usually runs 10 kilometers or swims 1,500 meters every morning, has breakfast and then writes, takes a break in the afternoon, and listens to music in the evening before going to bed. Keeping to a certain daily pattern seems to be key to maintaining their creativity.

This is an age where we have to structure our own lives. We would like to highlight this trend of people making an effort to keep to their own daily schedules with our next keyword "Routinize Yourself." Routines are usually actions and procedures that we undertake every day. The younger generations nowadays use the English term "routine" to describe a certain set of tasks and practices, such as study routines, exercise routines, and work routines. Activities at certain times of the day are often referred to as morning and evening routines. These routines are similar to habits in that they are repeatedly carried out at regular intervals but differ in that the former involves a more conscious effort to control one's way of life. Konan Technology's analysis of hashtags related to "habits" and "routines" showed that "habits" referred to "collective actions that were repeated consciously or subconsciously," whereas "routines" referred to "plans or a set of actions established with the aim of conscious repetition." While both keywords incorporate a sense of repetition, "routines" are attributed more to concrete planning. It also showed that references to "habits" are recently waning, while those to "routines" are steadily on the rise.

"Routinize Yourself" continues in the vein of the "Elevate Yourself업글인간" trend outlined in *Consumer Trend Insights 2020*. However, for these "routineers루틴이," such efforts in self-control do not just pertain to elevating or upgrading oneself as part of their self-management. Whereas those seeking to "elevate themselves" strive for a better version of themselves in the future, the values of these routineers run more along the vein of life resolutions, as in: "My life may be run-of-the-mill, but I will do my best at it." In a "Nano Society" where competition has intensified and hope grows dim, people are seeking to exercise self-control and relieve stress, thereby attaining the little joys in life. We will take a closer look at how routineers, as devotees of an ordinary and routine lifestyle, are making an effort to live their lives to the best of their abilities, and glimpse into a new way of life that is adapting to greater freedom.

How to Become a Routineer

We all wish to fill our day-to-day routines with worthwhile activities and become a true routineer, consistently carrying out these practices every day. However, it is easier said than done. The question is how to maintain one's routine and not give up mid-way. Routineers use the following strategies to stay on the straight and narrow.

1. Self-Constraint: Removing all potential hazards that may impede the process and setting up measures that will force themselves to stick to their routines.
2. Milestone Stamps: Seeking out a pacemaker that will encourage daily routines.
3. Retrospection: Placing value on the routine itself rather than rewards attained from the routines.

1. Placing constraints to complete tasks

As their primary tactic, routineers deliberately place themselves in an environment where they are forced to perform their routines, employing a strategy of "self-binding" or "self-constraint." Self-binding is a therapeutic tactic often used in the treatment of addictions, where subjects can practice restraint by setting up roadblocks between themselves and their addictions or addictive behavior. This effectively cages them in and prevents them from taking ill-advised action. It is a method to encourage oneself to carry out positive actions, leaving only the option to stick to one's routines.

Money is an effective medium of self-constraint and can be used as a "money-vation돈기부여 (a portmanteau 'money' and 'motivation')" strategy. Take for example the recent fad of taking "body profile pictures," or self-portrait photographs taken at a professional studio, to show off one's physique after months of consistent dieting and working out. Such photos were previously exclusive to celebrities and body-builders as promotional material. Nowadays more and more ordinary people are expressing an interest in commissioning such self-portraits. Why? The main purpose is of course to have for posterity images of themselves looking healthy and beautiful. There is also an additional factor for the younger generations: placing these pictures on their bucket list motivates them to work out consistently. And body profile pictures are not cheap. Renting out a studio and equipment such as cameras and lighting in addition to hiring a photographer, as well as expenses for hair, nails, makeup, tanning, and prop expenses can altogether easily run up more than 600,000 won ($506). Therefore, you force yourself to stick to a dietary and workout routine if you don't want to squander your hard-earned cash.

Courses that promise a partial refund on tuition fees, provided that the students faithfully attend and complete their lessons, are also a great source of motivation. One such example is the "Online Completion Program" at Day 1 Company데이원컴퍼니, which offers an extensive range of courses for adults including computer programming, data analysis, and marketing and creative directing. The education firm devised the program to encourage their students to keep up with their online courses until the very end. According to a study by U.S. venture capital firm Andreessen Horowitz, managing attendance for online courses is more difficult compared with face-to-face lessons, with the completion rate hovering around 3~7 percent. However, the rate for "Online Completion Programs" at Day 1 Company is roughly more than five times the average, standing at around 40 percent. The institute features other supportive measures for enrolled studies to not give up, such as providing daily and weekly education syllabi and one-on-one coaching services. Still, its "Online Completion Program" stands out as it sets weekly learning objectives or missions that students can achieve, after which they are offered a refund on part of their tuition. 94 percent of users have received refunds through this completion program, with their combined total reaching 850 million won ($720,000).

Time can also be a self-binding motivator. Forest is a productivity app that aims to help curb a user's smartphone addiction. It shows an image of your personal wooded forest that grows when you are not using your phone. If you are constantly on it, however, trees dry up and your woodland eventually dies. It allows the user to better manage their time and prevent smartphone addiction by turning its method into a game. The Time Timer is a product that is gaining a following among exam-taking students, forcing them to concentrate on the task at hand. Its 60-minute clock allows users to visualize the passage of time and is sometimes referred to as "the Google Timer" as staff at the IT giant often use it for meetings. Smartphone apps that help manage time are also gaining in popularity. The Visual Timer is an app similar to Time Timer that allows employees and students to check on how much time they spend completing tasks at work and at school.

2. Stamps to set the pace

Pacemakers often help marathon runners keep track of their progress by conveying a tangible point of reference. They never aim to break records or show outstanding running times themselves, but rather assist their athletes to do so. This is the second strategy that routineers often use: finding a pacemaker. We often find that we tend to study better when teachers are keeping watch, or that we focus better on tasks under the eagle eye of superiors at work, as if they are handing out stamps of approval.

Students try to take advantage of their digital environment to help them concentrate when attending online classes from home, as they must undertake assignments on their own as part of their self-directed learning process. The "study with me" tactic is one such example in which they turn on visual conferencing apps to watch each other studying as a type of quasi-surveillance. In August 2021, the Busanseo Middle School provided a self-directed learning program over the summer holidays on a strictly voluntary basis. 58 students signed up for the program, setting their own daily schedules for five study periods each day between 9 a.m. and 1 p.m. Each group consisting of seven or eight students followed their own study schedules from home under the watchful eye of a university student volunteer, observing one another through laptops or tablets. The images of other fellow students in the group, as well as the constant monitoring by the university student, helped them concentrate on their studies.

Apps that also help encourage complete strangers to accomplish their tasks are becoming increasingly popular. Yeolpumta열품타, an app with the acronym for "Passionate Timer열정을 품은 타이머," is a virtual study room for those who cannot physically go to libraries or study centers due to social distancing protocols. The app allows people with shared interests to form study groups. Active members include study groups formed by students from Korea, Sungkyunkwan, and Chung-Ang Universities, and those from specific majors including nursing or business administration, and even one that is based on Ravenclaw, the dormitory from the Harry Potter series that is home to some of the brightest and wisest students. Each group can accept up to 50 members, and competition is fierce during exam season to gain acceptance into the virtual study group of your choice. Each group set up their own regulations, with some stipulating members should log on and study for at least 10 hours a week, or face expulsion. Group members are privy to the study times and rankings of others, allowing themselves to set their own pace for hitting the books.

And as companies expanded teleworking, they too have introduced "stamps" to enhance concentration in their employees' work routines. "Bossware" or "tattleware" programs allow monitoring of employees, taking screenshots of staff at work, and sending data to management of employee log-on and log-off activity. Corporate management's use of remote monitoring tools such as ActivTrak, Teramind, and Time Doctor is rapidly surging amid the prolonged pandemic. And surprisingly, not all responses from employees subject to such scrutiny have been negative. According to a September 2021 report by British daily *The Guardian*, a survey showed that nearly three quarters of workers said their productivity would not be affected even with the knowledge their employer was monitoring them. Their positive response may be due to a support system that helps them focus on work on their own in an autonomous work environment.

3. Making every day count: retrospection

Recently, the term "retrospect" has been increasingly used among employees in the IT sector, instead of the word "review." The English word comes from Latin, "*retro + spectare*," meaning "backward + observe." The term is usually associated with memoires, recollection, and reminiscence. Still, in Korea, the word is regarded as a synonym for "review." However, there are obvious differences in their local usage. A "review" in Korea can be directly translated as an "examination," which aims to evaluate the initial aim versus the end result. A company often assesses the annual achievements of their staff or corporate performance using the key performance indicator, or KPI. On the other hand, "retrospect" indicates a literal look back on past actions, making note of what tasks were carried out at work, and what was learned. The emphasis is on the act of looking back itself, checking on what they got right, or what needs improvement, rather than taking measure of their success or whether they were able to accomplish set goals or not. It is similar to a journal entry in that it imbues meaning to each moment of one's day.

The final strategy used by routineers is looking back to find meaning in one's daily actions. The results gleaned from routines are not considered successes or failures. If we put pressure on ourselves every time we perform a routine, telling ourselves "I need to do this to lose *x*-number of pounds," or "I need to do that to boost my grades by a factor of n," we will ultimately lose interest in completing these routines. Setting goals such as reducing body fat by x percentage points or shedding x-number of pounds and achieving results is undoubtedly important. What is even more important is how much fun you are having in the process. Enjoying every moment of your exercise will naturally lead to positive results. The core value of retrospection also lies in finding meaning in daily mundane routines and patting yourself on the back for a job well done.

The rise in these "retrospective tribes회고족" has spawned a resurgence of a subgroup that focuses on decorating their organizers or daily planners. According to online bookstore and stationery seller Yes24, sales of organizer-related stationery, including writing tools, decorative stamps and tape, surged 61.9 percent in 2020 from the previous year, the biggest jump since the steady rise of such items in 2018. Decorating daily planners is the most basic of retrospective actions in that it provides an opportunity to look back on the day, giving yourself a gold star or a special sticker to mark a completed task or routine. Every box filled in your planner is a reward or a feather in your cap that provides the much-needed motivation to complete even more tasks and routines.

There are even apps that let you jot down your feelings at any point during the day. MOODA is a mood tracker and digital diary/planner app that allows the user to organize their moods and feelings of the day using nine emojis that say "Great!," "Peaceful," "Concerned," "Tired," or "Lovin' it." Once you input the emojis, the app offers words of encouragement or congratulations. Mooda creator and CEO Kim Ah-reum said she developed the app for her brother when he was going through a rough time at work, after reading an article that said recording one's emotions offers a sense of peace.

Background to the Rise of Routineers

The lifestyles of these routineers who try to make the best of an ordinary day is not a completely novel trend. Still, what we should note is the elevated emphasis placed on the value of daily, ordinary routines, and that routineers' values of creating their own structure in their lives are becoming more widely accepted. So, what is the reason behind their resurgence? We will take a contextualized look.

Enhanced degree of daily freedom

Case #1. A day in the life of an office worker
I take a quick shower immediately after getting up in the morning. I throw on my usual workwear, grab a light breakfast, then rush out to catch the bus. I doze off on the way to the office. A

hectic workday begins, only briefly interrupted by lunch, and I grab the bus back in the evening. I get home, order some dinner, slide into bed, and check the dates for my next holiday before falling asleep.

Case #2. A day in the life of a high school student
The morning alarm jolts me awake. I get cranky with my parents, griping that they didn't wake me earlier. I throw on my uniform and school bag, grabbing something to munch on as I rush out the door. After school ends, I join a group of friends heading to a cram school, drop by a nearby convenience store for a quick bite before heading to a private study room. I trudge back home late at night in a seemingly endless cycle that repeats for two semesters and two school breaks every year.

These were the usual pre-pandemic routines for many of us. It was an unchanging repetition of schooldays and semesters, or workdays interspaced with school breaks, vacations, or public holidays. The virus outbreak threw our familiar lives into chaos. Students attending online classes from home found it increasingly difficult to differentiate school days from school holidays. They only need to watch recorded lectures online within a given time frame and are not required to sit at their desks from 8 a.m. to 5 p.m. every day. Corporate workers feel that lines are blurring between workdays and weekends. It doesn't matter if they start their day at 9 or 10 a.m., so long as they complete their required tasks. Such conditions have boosted the level of freedom in their daily lives. They only need to set up their own schedules and show progress and results in their work. Keeping to a regular schedule of going to and from school or the office has become unnecessary.

The enhanced degree of freedom and autonomous planning do not stem solely from COVID-19. Society has been moving towards an enhanced level of freedom at school and at the workplace for quite some time. The official start of a five-day, 52-hour workweek exemplifies the trend, and the pandemic has even prompted discussions of a four-day workweek in some companies amid a rise in teleworking and telecommuting. The idea will likely gain a foothold in sectors that are looking for talented recruits, as some among the younger generations, who place more emphasis on finding the right balance between work and private life, value "spare time" more than a higher annual salary.

Such an enhanced degree of freedom has ironically heightened anxiety among some. The lack of structure in their daily routines has only increased their stress levels. They have begun to doubt whether they are properly managing their routines, fretting over carelessly throwing away valuable time. They feel uneasy in the fear that they are the only ones lagging, or that they are the only ones not living well. Such a loss of control is prompting them to try to reaffirm and regain their sense of control. They try to do this by striving to become routineers and pursue a somewhat structured lifestyle. Routineers, who are often described as compulsively productive, often try to max out their schedules because they find boredom more intolerable than idleness.

Spotlight on the little joys in life

According to Statistics Korea, the number of "discouraged workers" climbed to 583,000 as of June, up by 46,000 or 8.6 percent from a year earlier. "Discouraged workers" are defined as job seekers who tried to gain employment in the past year but have abandoned the search in the preceding four weeks due to a stagnant job market. It is the highest level since the agency began compiling data in 2014, and half of the discouraged workers consisted of people in their 20s and 30s. This is further evidence of the cutthroat competition among the younger generations amid a hiring freeze during the economic downturn triggered by the pandemic. The older generations, who suffered through dire hunger and poverty that followed the Korean War, may believe that the younger generations have little to complain about. However, the sense of depravation stemming from a lack of opportunity is acute among the youth of today.

Nobel Prize-winning Israeli cognitive psychologist Daniel Kahneman says most people are not interested in happiness, but rather "want to maximize their satisfaction with themselves and with their lives." According to Kahneman, the concept of happiness differs from that of satisfaction: happiness is a momentary experience that is fleeting, while satisfaction is a long-term feeling, built over time and based on achieving goals and building the kind of life you admire.

For example, spending time with friends helps to enhance immediate happiness, but it does not help to satisfy – and actually impedes – long-term goals, such as passing exams. Therefore, people are willing to forgo their "happiness of the present" for "success or life satisfaction in the distant future." However, in a period of stagnation where the future remains unclear, people value the little joys in life rather than anticipate a greater level of satisfaction in the future, as outlined in our chapter on the trend of "Small but Certain Happiness소확행" in the 2018 edition of *Consumer Trend Insights*. In a Nano Society where the future remains uncertain, hope grows dim, and people have come to pursue "the little joys in life" by concentrating on simple routines that grant immediate happiness.

Changing perceptions of "living the good life" have also put a bigger spotlight on these routineers. When Korea underwent rapid economic growth, "a successful life" was defined by people whose curricula vitae stretched for miles, listing phenomenal careers and achievements, or those whose garages resembled a showroom for imported vintage and limited-edition automobiles, or those who were renowned and well recognized through multiple TV appearances. By contrast, as Korea begins its transition into a more mature society from a developing one, its definition of "success" is changing from "wealth," "honor," and "stature," to "ordinary lives" and "normal routines." Ordinary office employees diligently carrying out their daily routines are emerging as the role models of today, and the formula for success is no longer a common ideal dictated by parents, friends, schools, or society; it is one that is established through one's own trajectory in life.

Outlook and Implications
— Happiness stems from diligence

Watering potted plants on your balcony; feeding and caring for your animal companions; cooking your daily meal; reading from a favorite book and jotting down phrases that particularly resonate with you; downloading and editing videos of your favorite celebrity in your style for your personal collection. These are some of the more run-of-the-mill activities that are trending these days as routineers do not seek to impress others, epitomizing the value of personal routines. These routineers show us that "happiness comes from diligence," an idea that may be all too obvious and yet difficult to adhere to.

Supporting consumer demand for establishing routines

So how can companies apply this trend to their operations? They need to acknowledge changing perceptions of routineers who seek to create and follow their own structured routines, and shrewdly make appropriate adjustments. For example, younger smartphone users make use of push notifications that pop up on their lock screens to constrain and motivate them to stick to their routines, much like jotting down to-do lists on sticky notes and attaching them to computer monitors. Users can also link push notifications to data searches. Newsbot뉴스봇 is Kakao Talk's news subscription service in which users can add the bot to their friends list on the messaging app. This allows news alerts to pop up on designated topics or "keywords," which comes in handy. For example, if you set "ESG" as a keyword, any news from web portals containing the term will appear as a notification from Newsbot's chat room. The users can also designate how the alerts appear: as daily briefings that appear once a day so they can browse through the list on their commute, or as immediate notifications that appear like instant headline alerts throughout the day. Recent trends also include newsletter services that help establish a routine. Mobile news apps such as NEWNEEK뉴닉 and financial newsletter app Uppity어피티, as well as platforms that introduce new products in the market, such as Alice Media앨리스 미디어, all send their subscribers summaries and information at no cost. They are services for which routineers can easily apply if they find them useful.

Applying "Routinize Yourself" to managing HR

From a business perspective, managers and staff members are internal customers. Therefore, they should take into account the ever-widening trend of routineers in managing their organization and human resources. Global streaming service giant Netflix is renowned for its corporate philosophy of "people over process" and "context, not control."

Netflix co-founder Reed Hastings, and co-author of *No Rules Rules: Netflix and the Culture of Reinvention*, defines the firm's culture as one where "No Rules Rules." The company encourages their staff to make independent decisions free of unwarranted process, which increases the chances of them making better and more responsible choices. For example, there are no rules on how many days their staff can take off. "Our vacation policy is 'take vacation.' We don't have any rules or forms around how many weeks per year," Hastings says in his book. It purposely exhibits confidence in its staff, supporting their decisions and granting them freedom, power, and information, and motivates them to behave responsibly.

Recently, local corporate culture has also been following the trend of ensuring independent freedom. Cheil Worldwide, the marketing arm of Samsung Group, was the first among domestic advertising agencies – a sector infamous for late-night sessions that carry over into the morning – to introduce the 52-hour work week. It recently began allowing two-hour lunch breaks to allow their staff to flexibly manage their hours. Employees make efficient use of their extended breaks to work out at the gym, or attend Chinese language study groups, or listen to online English courses. Encouraging such an autonomous culture stems from the company's confidence in their staff's voluntary and personalized routines. In other words, the spreading trend of routineers has enabled a self-directed culture at businesses, leading to improved results.

The trend of routineers is forcing us to reconsider fundamental assumptions made about human nature. According to the late Professor Douglas McGregor from the MIT Sloan School of Management, his Theory X and Theory Y on work motivation describe contrasting management models. Theory X holds that workers inherently have little ambition and avoid responsibility without proper supervision. His Theory Y, on the other hand, assumes that company staff are internally motivated, enjoy their jobs, and work to better themselves. Professor William Ouchi of the UCLA Anderson School of Management proposed his Theory Z, which gained recognition as a "Japanese management" style and attempts to supplement the X and Y theories, as it emphasizes fostering employee loyalty and unofficial control through stable long-term employment. Payment and welfare policies at most corporate entities are essentially based on Theory X and stem from the managers' lack of trust in workers. The COVID-19 outbreak initially posed the question of how to monitor staff and students working and attending classes from home.

Nevertheless, as we have observed, people do not necessarily give in to self-indulgence when given the freedom to organize their own schedules. They devise their own routines and voluntarily put in place external elements to help exercise self-control and manage themselves. As the saying goes, "life finds a way." The rise of the routineers is the answer that some of us have found to deal with the sudden freedom in our lives. The trend of routineers is evidence that trust among people has the potential to support structural management, school education, and even parental guidance. Humans instinctively seek to improve themselves, and thus we need to have faith in our basic nature to seek momentum to push ourselves forward when we are stuck in a rut. Only when we can rewrite the *modus operandi* to relationships based on trust can we create an entirely new culture and let it take root.

Connecting Together through Extended Presence

As the "untact" era becomes our new normal, Extended Presence Technology, which breaks through physical limitations of time and space and allows users to experience an actual presence through daily activities, is fast emerging as a core technological link between companies and their customers. It is a technology that encompasses advances that give shape to the reality-virtuality continuum, which allows us to expand our horizons by creating virtual spaces, stimulating various senses, and combining digital data with analog forms.

Critical properties of Extended Presence Technology include the coherent conscious perception of a multimodal sensory stimulus, sensory inputs that are perceived to be synchronous in time and space, and the experiential value attained through concentration by moving the body. What becomes key is the ability to persuade consumers into feeling that they have transcended themselves. A digital and segmented society, coupled with a global pandemic, has impeded our ability to find the "self" that stands out among others. Therefore, the ultimate goal of Extended Presence Technology should be to satiate the need to resolve the lack of presence in our daily lives and to retrieve a sense of self. Implementing Extended Presence Technology in business involves activities that allow consumers to immerse themselves in the experience, as well as a careful consideration of the response they wish to evoke in their customers with regards to their firm, products and services – areas that require candid and immediate feedback. In an era where most aspects of our lives transcend reality, the core to the greatest technological capabilities that will allow companies to hold onto their customers will lie in the firm that stands out in consumer expectations through Extended Presence Technology.

Case #1. *A new star is taking the world of advertising by storm. After her sensational debut as spokesmodel for Shinhan Life Insurance, she has clinched eight additional commercial contracts and more than a hundred corporate sponsorships. We are of course referring to "Rozy," Sidus Studio X's virtual influencer. The perennial 22-year-old will never age, and as she will never suffer from obsessive stalker fans, the advertising sector has high expectations for the virtual star.*

Astounding advances in modern science and technology has turned what was only once imaginable into virtual reality. The nation's first cyber singer "Adam" burst onto the scene back in 1998. The five-foot-ten, 150-pound idol, who apparently loved kimchi stew, was based on a distinctive concept. However, he quickly faded into obscurity as he was clearly a computer-generated character. Fast forward more than two decades, and we are now living in a new age. Rozy has been joined by other virtual models and influencers, such as Lotte Homeshopping's "Lucy" and LG Electronics' "Kim Reah," who are gaining a growing following.

So, what are the differences between Adam and Rozy? How was she able to overcome the seemingly impenetrable barrier after some two decades? The key to Rozy's success may lie in her "presence," that is, in how realistically developers can represent her in a virtual space. If the virtual world of the past only imitated reality, the "virtuality" of today can literally represent "real" presence. And as science and technology were already on the cusp of rendering limitations in time and space irrelevant, COVID-19 further swept away psychological barriers of time and space. *Consumer Trend Insights 2022* dubs this trend "Extended Presence Technology," which overcomes the physical limitations of time and space in an era where the "untact," or non-contact, lifestyle has become our new normal. The keyword encompasses all aspects of technology that creates virtual spaces, stimulates a wide range of senses, and combines digital and analog forms, helping expand the overall spectrum of our lived experiences.

The term "presence" can be defined as "a sense of being there실재감." It is a subjective cognitive process and differs from merely "existing실재實在." For example, even if two people exist in and share the same space, their sense of "presence" can vary depending on their individual awareness of the situation. Therefore, Extended Presence Technology is not a technical measure of how close to reality something is, but rather a question of perception as to how much consumers can immerse themselves in an experience and believe that it is actually real.

A metaverse that makes virtuality a reality; social media that supports multimodal senses; live commerce sales that interact vivaciously with consumers; media façades that breathe new life into offline areas. Extended Presence Technology is no longer limited to the big screen in blockbuster science fiction movies or imaginable only in some distant future. It is a clear and present technology that is fast progressing even now. It is also quickly becoming a major technology that can bring unlimited diversity to consumer platforms. Consumers are able to perceive a new kind of awareness of themselves through Extended Presence Technology, stepping beyond the boundaries of commerce, and experience a seamlessly interlaced interaction between the virtual and reality. In an era where most sectors are transcending reality, the core to technological capacity lies in whoever can believably actualize extended presence.

Extended Presence Technology: Three Critical Properties

As seen in the introduction, Extended Presence Technology is taking hold, not just as an element of entertainment but also as a technology that can be put to practical use in our lives and in the corporate sector. So, what kind of technical properties does it need to maximize applicability? What kind of technology do consumers require to become aware of the presence of virtuality? The three key properties consist of multimodal sensory interaction, synchronicity, and experientiality.

1. Multimodal sensory interaction

Multimodal senses refer to the various human senses and the relation between them. Human beings perceive others or objects through a combination of their five senses. They interact among themselves as well as provide stimulus to each other through association.

Synesthesia demonstrates the dynamic associations between the senses, as stimulating one sense can trigger involuntary reactions of the other senses. The oddity can result in misinterpretation of the senses, but also lead to a favorable response. Consumers can accept such sensory deviations as novel, interesting, and original.

One such example is a commercial for Haribo gummies, in which a group of men and women dressed in executive suits are seated around a conference table. Holding a gummy bear of their choice, each of them starts talking about their favorite color or flavor with glee, but their voices are dubbed by five-year-olds, complete with lisps and childlike mannerisms. The sensory incongruity forces consumers to take a closer look and reminds them of the joy experienced as children when they first tasted gummy bears. The more diverse the sensory levels, the more vested consumers become in the products.

There is a wide range of examples of the use of multimodal sensory experiences in the world of business. Online shopping platform Musinsa opened a flagship store in the hip Hongdae area of Seoul in May 2021. The shop sported optical stimulations in its spiral staircase, tempered designs, and display cases in muted colors, and offered music that was pleasant to listen to. It was filled with plant-based fragrances such as patchouli drenched in dew fresh from the forest, the carefree beauty of jasmine, the spicy allure of carnations, the warmth of amber, and the raw charm of vetiver oil that satisfied the olfactory senses. In other words, Musinsa made use of sensory stimulation to make an impression of its brand on their customers and to present their corporate identity as being "in pursuit of unwavering values in the everchanging cycle of time."

There are also specific senses that have a greater impact compared to others. We call this "sensory dominance." We can find a leading example at mega multiplexes that use a technology that allows the sense of hearing to overwhelm the eyes. The Dolby Atmos system, found in many cineplexes, is sometimes called "moving audio" because it allows moviegoers to experience sound that transforms into motion. The system involves creating a sound dome by placing a myriad of different audio channels on the ceiling, walls, and the floor, thus allowing for intricate programming that allows sounds to emanate from certain angles or wash over the audience in a sweeping motion. This allows cinephiles to immerse themselves in the movie as though they were within them.

2. Synchronicity:
Perception of immediate and concurrent engagement

The second property of Extended Presence Technology is synchronicity – allowing consumers to feel the immediacy of something as though it were taking place in the present moment. We can find a good example in real-time strategy, or RTS, games such as the StarCraft series by Blizzard. Unlike turn-based strategy games, RTS gamers log on at the same time to play with one another, granting them a heightened sense of extended presence. As there is a time limit for each round, players are forced to concentrate, which enhances their immersion.

Live commerce shopping, which allows vendors to sell their wares through livestreams on social media or video sharing platforms, is a meeting of synchronicity and online consumer patterns. The vendor may prepare a script before going on air, but much of the broadcast is made up of the shopping host interacting with potential buyers who join the broadcast online. Shoppers who enter these streams chat with the hosts through messages for various reasons that include (a) obtaining information, (b) having a conversation with the hosts, or (c) creating funny content, and through these interactions vendors and hosts help create a lively online market by responding in real time. In its early days, farmers and small businesses created a niche market by selling their own products and produce such as food and clothing at cheap prices to acquire new sales channels. It has now grown into a proper retail channel that sells anything from luxury items like giant household appliances, or even intangible goods like travel and leisure packages and online courses. The simultaneous nature of live commerce shopping acts as a medium that narrows the psychological divide between vendors and consumers, bringing them closer together. This is because human beings communicate not just through words but also through muscle movement including gestures and expressions, as well as through the clothes they wear and how they wear them.

3. Experientiality: Substituting movement in real life

The final property of Extended Presence Technology is grabbing consumers' attention by prompting them to move their bodies. Lost Ark, a popular animated massively multiplayer online role-playing game (ARPG or MMORPG), joined hands with fast food franchise Mom's Touch맘스터치 to launch an interesting marketing event in July 2021. If the gamer visited a Mom's Touch within the online game world and ordered a virtual chicken set, the gamer's character gained higher stats. And during the same period, if the gamer visited a nearby outlet of Mom's Touch in the real world, they could order chicken set menus named after Lost Ark characters and receive item coupons they could redeem in the virtual game world. And as their gaming characters leveled up by eating virtual chicken dinners, so did the gamers in the real world, creating an experiential event through the Extended Presence Technology.

The technology is even more pronounced in the field of education, allowing students to actively take part and stimulate their interest. Remote learning and homeschooling constrained the scope of laboratory classes and practical training, which enhanced interest in tools and realistic content that provided vivid online learning. VISANG, which began as a publishing company, was one of the first in the industry to branch out into educational content and technology. The use of its virtual and augmented reality content in the April-June period in 2020 soared 10 times from the previous quarter of January-March. Its VR content on geological surveys that allowed users to browse through virtual digs and museums to look at digital fossils, rocks, and minerals, saw views jump 10.5-fold, while access to its AR science lab, which allows subscribers to operate lab tools and equipment in a virtual environment, increased 8.1-fold over the cited period.

The Role of Extended Presence Technology

What is the function of Extended Presence Technology? In other words, what kind of sensory experience does it provide consumers? We can boil this down to one word: transcendence초월超越. It signifies the act of overcoming limitations and can also mean an act of competition by adding a higher tier above an object. Extended Presence Technology allows us to transcend our senses as well as time and space. We will take a closer look at industrial applications of the Extended Presence Technology through such transcendent experiences.

Transcending the limitations of the five senses

Firstly, transcending the senses means to overcome the limit of the five senses – in other words, replacing how we perceive human sensations. Physical stimulations from our environment are transmitted through the eyes, ears, nose, tongue, and skin through neurotransmitters to ultimately trigger changes in the brain. Such changes are what we know as senses. In other words, the five senses perceived by human beings are ultimately a reaction from the brain. Therefore, if we can inject electric signals to substitute physical stimulation or trigger neural transmissions, we can be fooled into thinking we can taste or smell certain foods without the corresponding stimulation. If such attempts are successful, we will be able to attain a wide range of sensory experiences anywhere and anytime.

Dr. Aradhna Krishna, a professor of marketing at the University of Michigan Ross School of Business, defines sensory marketing as one that "engages the consumers' senses and affects their perception, judgment, and behavior." And, similarly, Extended Presence Technology induces consumers to transcend their general senses, affecting their perception, judgment, and behavior. Such technology has a wide range of uses. Malaysia's Imagineering Institute based in Johor combines imagination with engineering, as its name suggests, and works to make into reality what we could only previously imagine. Its Digital Smell Interface stimulates olfactory neural receptors using faint electrical signals, simulating the perception of specific smells. If this technology can be adapted for commercial use, it will allow online shopping platforms and food delivery apps to break free of limitations, especially in the field of food retail and services.

Transcending time and space:
Past and future, beyond spatial boundaries

Extended Presence Technology also allows people to transcend the ultimate boundaries of time and space. Time in particular can never flow in reverse. However, Extended Presence Technology allows us to surpass the boundaries of the time continuum. And because what happened specifically in the past cannot be replaced, precious moments can be created.

Cheil Worldwide's German affiliate created VR marketing content in 2015 for Samsung called "VR The Future" to celebrate the 25th anniversary of Germany's reunification, allowing users to don VR headsets to appreciate and experience iconic German landmarks from different eras across the country.

In 2020, the National Research Institute of Cultural Heritage, which operates under South Korea's Cultural Heritage Administration, collaborated with the city of Gyeongju, which served as the capital during the Silla Dynasty for nearly a millennium until the end of the 10th century. They virtually recreated part of the legendary Hwangnyongsa황룡사, a Buddhist temple that dates back to the 7th century and of which only massive foundation stones remain today. Users can hold a tablet PC to view a virtual recreation using real-time marker-based camera location tracking technology, as well as view the various artifacts found on the site.

China Grand Canal Museum in Yangzhou, which opened to the public in June 2021, uses immersive interactive technology to allow visitors to explore the canal and appreciate the scenery of its thousand-year history within the museum's premises. The massive museum complex itself is surrounded by water and consists of a four-story building in the shape of a ship with a mast which is actually a 100-meter (328-feet) pagoda. The museum has incorporated interactive virtual media that allows visitors to view relics found in the world's longest and oldest canal and its tributaries, a burial mound in the shape of ships dating back to the Tang dynasty, as well as kiln sites from the Song dynasty. The museum succeeded in virtually recreating the grandeur of giant marine vessels and details of an ancient city through digital media, combining multiple time periods stretching back into the past and moving forward in time to the present, which provides an immersive experiential area displaying numerous sections of the canal on fully interactive touchscreens and through augmented reality and carefully placed lighting.

Applying extended presence technology to business

The most important aspect in businesses applying Extended Presence Technology is maintaining their unique corporate values. Moreover, firms need to continue mulling over how to enhance their customers' lives in the midst of rapidly changing environments. Companies can gain familiar footing with consumers only when customers can identify corporate goals that shine through the deluge of high-tech artificial technology. And it is also better to emphasize the added value of the product than focus on the specific technology used.

The ultimate goal of Extended Presence Technology is to improve the lives of their customers. A primary example is virtual reality therapy (VRT). We are now able to treat post-traumatic stress disorder (PTSD), phobias, pain, and alcoholism by creating mixed realities through haptic rendering technology. Local companies and medical corporations are also actively making use of a wide range of relevant technologies.

Also worth noting are developments in the AI smart display market. Google's Nest Hub Max and Amazon's Echo Show are among some of the AI smart displays making inroads in the market, which provide multisensory content closely linked to consumers' daily lives. What is remarkable is that these AI devices, which consumers initially used as tools to look up information, are evolving along with the development of artificial intelligence. AI smart displays are not only providing information via text but are now able to articulate the results of their findings, providing an amalgamation of audio and visual data. And if we add elements of augmented reality such as measuring tools, cooking timers, and recipe videos, we have our own personal cooking instructor providing step-by-step instructions on preparing a complicated meal. This is an ideal way in which a company can meet the needs of its customers through technology, providing them with a realistic presence by doing what it does best.

Metaverse:
Blurring the line between the virtual and real world

"Metaverse" refers to an expanded virtual world and is a portmanteau of "meta," meaning transcendence or virtual, and "universe." It is a three-dimensional virtual world, moving beyond the cyber social space of the past that was best represented by the online game Second Life. It offers realistic renderings or imitations of the five sense, that makes it almost impossible to differentiate from the real world. In the metaverse, people can manufacture or trade goods and assets, giving birth to a virtual economy. Many activities that are conducted in the real world, such as education, entertainment, and commerce are also taking place in the metaverse.

The virtual world of the metaverse needs to anchor itself to the real world, and even partially replace reality. In that sense "Gather" is regarded as a quintessential metaverse platform. Developed by U.S. startup Gather Presence, it provides an online pixelated space that allows multiple users to feel as though they are working together in an online office. This has been a breath of fresh air for those weary of endless series of video conference calls. Once you enter Gather, you are assigned stumpy pixelated avatars, a throwback to RPG characters from decades-old RPG games such as the beloved Zelda or Final Fantasy series. However, unlike other metaverse platforms, you do not communicate through your avatar but click on another person's avatar, which pops up an actual image of the person sitting at their desks as if they are on a conference call. It supports audio communication and provides other office and operational support channels. One can use a myriad of cookie cutter conference rooms and lecture halls or other spaces where employees can relax or enjoy games together.

LG Display held its online training sessions for 200 new employees on Gather in the first half of 2020. A survey conducted after the session showed that 91 percent of respondents felt that it was an effective networking tool. ZIGBANG직방, a real estate app operator which completely eliminated physical offices and began a remote working system from early 2021, also opened its online offices on Gather. As not only startups but also leading global corporations are jumping on the metaverse wagon, Facebook's moves have been particularly astounding. In October 2021, its CEO Mark Zuckerberg, an avid proponent of the metaverse, introduced his concept of the "infinite office," saying that his company will make a transition into a metaverse company from a mobile internet firm in the next five to seven years, rebranding its company as "Meta" or "Meta Platforms." It aims to maximize extended presence through the development of its AR glasses that will help eliminate the boundary between actual and virtual reality, allowing users to project virtual images onto the real world.

Outlook and Implications
— Extended Presence Technology as a methodical tool

Students from rival universities in the Gwangjin District of Seoul held an unconventional competition in June 2021 to determine which group was superior. Extracurricular activity groups at Konkuk and Sejong Universities held online competitions to breathe some life back into their stagnant campus lives since the viral outbreak. The so-called "Battle for Gwangjin District" involved numerous events including e-sport matches, programming and coding jams, hip-hop/rap diss battles, as well as a battle of the bands, to determine who would emerge as the "ruler" of various sections of the district, with each section won sporting their university pennants or colors. These battles were waged on- and offline (with only online spectators), and the results were displayed on a digital map. However, as the backdrop to these events took place in a virtual world that depicted their actual neighborhood, the students fiercely dueled for superiority, becoming completely immersed in the process. And as word of the competition spread through social media, their stylishly edited diss battle videos racked up more than 40,000 views. It was an online campus festival – a way for students to make up for what they had lost and let off frustrations pent up during two consecutive years of online lectures, allowing them to partially reclaim a sense of camaraderie and fellowship through the extended presence of university life.

As the above clearly shows, the key to Extended Presence Technology lies in maintaining and augmenting the user's actual and realistic enjoyment, even within the confines of virtual space. In a digital world, we need to preserve analog values as well. The "untact" trend of the COVID-19 era has led to a deficiency in extended presence, which people are coming to desire in modern society. As society becomes more segmented in the midst of a digital transition, companies must be able to satisfy their customers' needs by resolving this deficiency and to help them reclaim a fuller sense of their selves. Companies need a better understanding of emotions and psychology as well as technology to allow consumers to appreciate the sincerity of others who are not physically next to them.

For example, one of the reasons why people feel a "familiarity" with virtual influencer Rozy is that she is "far from perfect" and only "seems somewhat human." Some even say that she is far from beautiful. As a virtual character, developers could have made her as perfectly symmetrical or pleasing to the eye as they wished. However, they chose to include flaws and defects and left room for future improvement. According to an official from Rozy's creator Sidus Studio X, they wanted a face with character and mystery rather than one that was flawless. They wanted to mitigate a sense of the uncanny valley – the feeling of unease, detachment, or even revulsion when looking at a highly realistic face.

Their true focus lay not in Rozy's appearance but in her lifestyle. With her default age forever at 22, and with interests such as world travel, yoga, running, fashion and an eco-friendly lifestyle, her character was defined as "outgoing," "carefree," and "sociable." She gained an affinity with millennials and Gen Zers through her active involvement in social issues, such as taking part in zero-waste challenges. What is important is to induce a feeling of kinship and empathy with others by creating unique worldviews. As new horizons open in high-tech fields such as the metaverse, which is rapidly gaining a foothold, companies may feel tempted to hastily lure consumers' attention with novel technology. However, a sudden introduction of new tech branching out into new businesses may only strain existing capacity and wear out staff resources.

Rather than fall prey to complex methodologies, firms need to devise strategies that streamline and rearrange the existing framework to stick to the basics and enhance customers' immersion and their sense of extended presence. If corporations choose to develop new businesses and neglect customer relations, consumers, who already feel disassociated amid a lack of connection, will only remain as bystanders or observers. Companies need to focus on beefing up their networking abilities to connect with consumers and widen the pool in order to secure them as clients.

Extended Presence Technology is no longer a jaw-dropping novelty only seen in science fiction movies that depict a distant future. It provides a sense of interacting with or bumping into others, allowing us to transcend our senses, break through the limits of time and space, and offer an opportunity to experience synchronous multimodal stimulation of companies' products and services. Extended Presence Technology is a methodical tool that allows a business to take a step closer to their customers' daily lives. If the corporate sector succeeds in making use of Extended Presence Technology to erase limitations, transcending the senses, as well as time and space, it will surely be able to meet their customers' needs to reclaim their identities that have been increasingly fading in the real world. As we tackle our semi-compulsory non-contact era, we anticipate that the most positive outcome of Extended Presence Technology will be to resolve our sense of isolation brought on by the "Nano Society."

Actualizing Consumer Power – 'Like Commerce'

The number of "likes" sways our purchase decisions. The long-held paradigm of producers manufacturing goods and consumers buying them from retailers is shifting. Consumers are pioneering a new frontier in which they independently plan, design, manufacture, and sell products themselves. We call this consumer-driven retail process "Like Commerce," in that it begins with the number of likes received from other consumers.

"Like Commerce" is a demand-driven market that requires demand chain management (DCM), in contrast to the more traditional manufacturer-driven paradigm that focuses on supply chain management (SCM).

We live in an age where we no longer have to physically get up to go shop but rather make purchases anytime and anywhere with the tap of a finger while scrolling through searches or updated posts. Moreover, "Like Commerce" has emerged as a viable side job for many people after losing their jobs or having to find alternate sources of income during the COVID-19-triggered recession, and as we increase our non-contact interactions. An increasing number of customers are basing their purchase choices more on what is "distinctive" rather than on what is of "better quality." Consumers are opening their wallets for goods they've given "likes" to because they feel that they are "quite me," rather than because they are better than the previous models or different from all other alternatives offered in the market. "What goods suit me best?" is a question that retailers of the future will have to answer.

"If you have a solid base of a thousand followers, it's enough to set up your own business."

You no longer need to rack up large numbers to succeed in business. Nor do you need a $100,000 investment or a clientele of 100,000. All you need are 1,000 loyal followers who will buy anything that you churn out. They will travel hundreds of kilometers just to hear you sing, and if you publish a book, they will buy every edition from hardcovers and paperbacks to audio books.

Kevin Kelly, who is a guest writer in Tim Ferriss's *New York Times* bestseller *Tools of Titans: The Tactics, Routines, and Habits of Billionaires*, offered his thoughts on the dynamics of online businesses of today. If you have a thousand loyal followers – or "true fans," as he calls them – that "like" your content, they can become a source of income.

Fans and followers of specific brands have always been a cornerstone of a business. The 2020 edition of *Consumer Trend Insights* outlined the emergence of "fan-sumers" in a chapter called "You're With Us." Still, the number of followers you need to run a business has drastically declined recently from 100,000 to a mere 1,000. As the pace of development in digital technology accelerates, one of the key factors to a successful business has become less rigid. And such changes are causing a domino effect in the structure of industries.

In the past, a complex network ran from the manufacturer to the producer, with mass production and mass consumption being key to creating profit that exceeded costs. And due to exorbitant initial investment costs to set up manufacturing facilities and distribution networks, manufacturing-based operations had been exclusive to giant businesses, creating "a league of their own." Such a structure was repeated in the e-commerce market. Initial investments may have greatly diminished, but nevertheless companies that were able to secure a large number of users through cut-throat price competition obviously had an advantage over others. This is because giant shopping platforms led the charge in creating new markets.

The Rise of a New Retail Paradigm

There has been a decided shift in the conventional market's mass production-mass consumption paradigm. Anyone with a base of loyal followers can now start their own business.

The market is undergoing a realignment in which anyone with consumer support can manufacture, sell, and distribute their wares.

The three major forms of the new retail dynamic are listed below:

1. C2C (Consumer to Consumer): An individual content creator garners sufficient likes and, based on those numbers, places an order under an ODM (original design manufacturer) contract and sells them through a retail specialist.

2. D2C (Direct to Consumer): The manufacturer sometimes sells goods directly to customers by setting up its own store. The company analyzes data to estimate the number of likes it may receive from consumers, setting up its own retail outlet to cut down on distribution costs.

3. H2H (Human to Human): The maker receives orders in the form of likes to arrange a group purchase or pre-orders for brand-new products, thereby cutting down on production costs and reducing the risk of storage expenses.

And since this relatively new process begins from receiving "likes," we would like to dub this process "Like Commerce." In other words, "Like Commerce" refers to all types of new online retail based on customer preferences. The Like Commerce market is also a springboard for the future of retail with limitless growth potential. E-commerce, or what can be regarded as "online shopping ver. 1.0," emerged from the earlier days of the internet. Consumers began to browse for products that they wanted to buy online. Therefore, search engines became key factors to gaining a competitive edge.

Consumer feedback was the next important factor. Reviews of product purchases have become a must to back up online sales, as most transactions took place without any person-to-person contact. Online malls and platforms that excelled in these features became trailblazers and were able to corner the market. And as giant shopping platforms that were able to draw a large number of customers have become industry leaders in the business-to-consumer (B2C) model, the key factor to their success has been how they can lure the most customers through cheaper prices. And supply chain management (SCM) becomes important to maximize profits through cost-cutting measures. In an open platform, vendors become sellers, putting their products for sale on consignment as an intermediary in the chain.

By contrast, Like Commerce can be viewed as "online shopping ver. 2.0," bringing together consumer preferences and creating a new business model. In this stage, concepts such as B2B and B2C become meaningless. They take a wide range of forms from Consumer to Consumer (C2C), Direct to Consumer (D2C), to Human to Human (H2H), with person-to-person trade becoming a key factor. Anyone who can identify consumer preferences in a timely manner can have the upper hand in the market. The seller takes on the role of an overseer or strategist rather than a seller, as anyone can become a vendor, distributor, or manufacturer. Individuals who are both vendors and consumers create their own brands and take part in the manufacturing process. And in this format, bringing together customers that are scattered all over the place through demand chain management (DCM) is key. Sellers also have to maximize their customers' experiences to maintain a competitive edge. So, what is more important is not how many customers they are able to secure but rather how passionate the followers are about the goods the vendor put up for sale.

Like Commerce is a new paradigm in online retail. There are structural changes afoot in a market previously dominated by online shopping malls and platforms, as well as in their points of contact with customers. And at its center are the "likes" that vendors must garner from consumers. Let's take a closer look at the three business models that represent Like Commerce as an alternative retail structure, along with the expansion of the "untact" market amidst an extended pandemic.

Like Commerce: Three Business Models

1. C2C: Planning a private business

Setting up small private enterprises has never been easier. To start off, there are no physical limitations to setting up private businesses online. Conventional retailers are often bound by limited market territory, but such constraints don't exist on the internet. In fact, small operations often turn to social media platforms, creating unique content to appeal to consumers. Like Commerce continues in the vein of a trend outlined in our 2019 edition of *Consumer Trend Insights* in the chapter called "Invite to the 'Cell Market,'" in that it has greatly expanded opportunities for small-scale enterprises. That being said, it surpasses the Cell Market as it encompasses the whole value chain from planning to manufacturing, marketing, sales operations, and logistics. In Cell Markets, which are rooted in social media operations, most influencers sold their products in the form of group purchases. Group purchasing was a system favored by sellers as it allowed them to measure the exact demand for the goods, place orders, and sell the goods, allowing the vendor to cut down on storage expenses. The influencer's promotional ability is key to the success of a Cell Market. In fact, the rise and reach of influencers in the market seem to know no bounds. Up until a few years ago, images and cutouts of famous TV celebrities and movie stars adorned store windows and displays promoting cosmetics or food and beverages. Recently, influencers are taking over the role of main spokesmodels.

These social media celebrities have managed to take yet another giant step through the consumer to consumer (C2C) model of Like Commerce. Previously, influencers, armed with their great sway over followers, used to buy products in bulk and review them or make content to promote them for later sale. However, they have now begun to plan and produce as well as distribute and promote their own merchandise. In other words, this denotes a significant expansion in the scope of value chain creation. And it has simultaneously led to other issues such as manufacturing and distribution costs and the concern over one's stock of products. And to hedge some of these risks, vendors often look for reliable partners. Thankfully, there are various companies that have been able to meet the needs of these fledgling entrepreneurs. In other words, we are seeing the growth of an ecosystem to support Like Commerce, focusing on small-scale businesses. This is prompting a rise in partner firms for private entrepreneurs that can handle many aspects such as production, logistics, as well as sales operations.

Companies that specialize as original design manufacturers (ODM) are playing a key role in the market. Cosmetics companies in particular have shown stellar performance in their ODM operations, with many of them lowering their minimum order quantity (MOQ) requirements. Whereas ODMs usually manufacture products for major cosmetic brands by the tens of thousands, they have adjusted their practices for one-person business brands to accommodate "a wide range of smaller quantities." For example, COSMAX, which specializes as a cosmetics ODM, offers a "Micro-branding Launch" package that can handle a quantity of just 1,000. Creating a private cosmetics brand through ODMs allows vendors to lower development and fabrication costs.

Promoting that these independent brands were manufactured at facilities that cater to giant cosmetics firms can bolster consumer confidence. Kolmar Korea and COSMAX and other cosmetics makers list top brands such as Amorepacific and LG Household & Healthcare, as well as global giants such as L'Oréal and Shiseido, among their clients. As such, influencers can concentrate on sales and marketing while entrusting ODMs with planning, development, and production, thereby alleviating the burdens of the manufacturing process. These advantages have prompted a recent growth spurt in the cosmetics ODM market. According to a Global Industry Analysts (GIA) report, the global ODM market is expected to nearly double to $10 billion by 2027 from $5.5 billion in 2020. Dongdaemun Poomgo동대문 품고, which caters exclusively to retail clothing vendors by offering them a "fulfillment service," acts as their proxy in the shipping process, taking care of various steps such as checking stock, scanning for defects, packaging, and delivery. And with these specialized companies taking care of logistical issues, small businesses can enhance operational efficiency by keeping an accurate account of their stock, as well as by reducing the rate of defective and returned products.

In addition to beauty and fashion products, there are now partners that specialize in fresh produce and perishables that need to be delivered at low or freezing temperature. FASSTO파스토, works closely with e-commerce platforms, offering a comprehensive delivery system that automatically compiles orders, designates delivery tracking numbers, and ships out packages. The firm has kept with delivery trends and is preparing same-day or early morning deliveries, which are expected to help businesses that provide simple meals such as salads and lunch boxes.

And finally, there are other partner companies that can provide administrative expertise that small operations often find daunting, including filing taxes, taking online orders, and managing customers. For example, SamJjeomSam삼쩜삼, an AI-based corporate tax accounting service, gives clients an estimate of expected tax refunds if you input your mobile phone number and your login ID with the nation's tax administration service Hometax. It also provides a one-stop service in corporate tax accounting from filing general income taxes to receiving tax returns. INPOCK인포크, a platform for influencers, provides clients with sale solutions through its "INPOCK Store," helping them sell their wares more easily on social media.

2. D2C: Manufacturers reach out directly to buyers

Hyundai Motor Company made headlines when it became the first automaker to introduce a direct to consumer (D2C) sales channel in the domestic market. The nation's top carmaker agreed to sell exclusively online its entry-level SUVs "Casper," the first line to roll out this year as part of its collaborative project with labor unions and the city of Gwangju. The move was a resounding success, racking up pre-orders of 18,940 units on the first day alone, a record for the company's internal combustion engine brands, and far outstripped its 12,000-unit production target for the year. Total pre-orders reached nearly 25,000, even before they came off the assembly line, including one from President Moon Jae-in. The tally exceeded that of the 6th generation facelift of its luxury sedan Grandeur, more commonly known as "Azera" overseas, back in November 2019, which stood at 17,294 on the first day. The new mini-SUV possesses various standout features, but industry observers have noted that the D2C model helped enhance buyer convenience.

Manufacturers' forays into the D2C model began in the U.S. Ever since the departure of global sports giant Nike from Amazon and the subsequent success of its own online mall, the D2C model has become a viable next generation e-commerce strategy. The greatest advantage of the D2C model is that it can retain valuable data on its customers. Manufacturers can collate real-time data on consumer patterns through its online malls, reflecting it in new lines currently in development or even pulling off more personalized marketing strategies. D2C is an attractive option for management as lower distribution costs lead to larger profit margins, as well as improving customers' brand experience.

South Korean companies are also following suit by opening their own online malls. Hy Company, better known by its former name "Korea Yakult," recently redesigned its online mall Fredit프레딧, featuring dairy products, fresh produce, and health supplements, as well as cosmetics, detergents, bath products, household goods, child-friendly items, and eco-friendly lines to cater to vegan and organic conscious customers. The number of online mall members topped 1 million in 2021 from 680,000 the previous year. Clothing manufacturer Handsome Corp.한섬 also beefed up its online shopping mall "The Handsome," with accrued sales jumping by 67 percent as of the end of the third quarter compared with a year earlier. This prompted Handsome to boost its D2C channel, setting up its logistics base "Smart On Center" in Icheon, located southeast of Seoul, dedicated to its online mall.

The expansion of the D2C business model has also

provided a welcome opportunity for companies that offer shopping mall proxy services. Industry leaders include Korea's Cafe24 and Canadian multinational service provider Shopify. The latter offers e-commerce solutions that provide software to help companies run online mall operations. Solutions to issues such as setting up and managing its website, compiling and managing customer data, merchandise marketing, and processing credit card and other payments are available through Shopify. Those who use such services can easily set up online shopping malls, establish one's brand, and obtain valuable customer data, without any IT expertise.

3. H2H: Securing contact points with consumers

When customers express their approval, their accrued "likes" result in a crowd that wields great power. Distributors who have taken notice are making use of the trend to create new value. The so-called human to human (H2H) model is one that links people to other people, brings together manufacturer and buyer, or gathers individual buyers based on their shared preferences. There are three methods to the H2H model:

1. Production and sales on-demand: Verify demand, in a similar fashion to crowdfunding, and begin to manufacture the product once demand occurs.

2. Developing unique business models: Focus on a specific category based on consumer preferences to provide distinctive services.
3. Creating a business model based on "likes": Collate the amount of "likes" from a wide range of consumers at the development stage of a product or service to create a business model.

A prime example of the H2H model is crowdfunding in which a preliminary version of a new product is sold to gauge initial responses before an official release in the market. Manufacturers can kill two birds with one stone: they can launch a brand-new product and at the same time create buzz to promote the product. Wadiz와디즈, a platform that specializes in crowdfunding, is a quintessential H2H business model. As we can see in how Wadiz uses the terms "maker메이커" and "supporter서포터" instead of "seller" and "buyer," the dynamics between manufacturer and purchaser are more along the lines of funder or sponsor. Supporters not only provide funding but also take on a more active role by leaving messages to encourage the makers and share promotional product pages and posts onto their own social media accounts. Supporters take time to read the story on how the products were created and empathize with the philosophy behind the brand. Lesser-known independent brands find the platform useful in meeting loyal customers at the launch of their products. If a project is successful, they can add a tagline in the future, as in "succeeded in raising such-and-such amount of funding through Wadiz (or Kakao Makers)," which in itself is another appealing factor of these promotional platforms. Analysts point out that supporters are most interested in products that have yet to be officially released in the market, and those that have a unique story and value behind their goods receive positive responses.

Focusing on a specific category of their choice helps maximize the H2H model. If a group of like-minded supporters gathers to fund the product, profit will naturally ensue. Users of the cleaning, renovation, and home interior app OHouse오늘의집, operated by Bucketplace버킷플레이스, is a singular service that organically combines content, community, and commerce. As members share pictures of their space, boasting their acumen for colors, designs, and sophisticated tastes, other users take note and refer to the pictures when changing their own interior, which leads to purchases of relevant wares available through the platform. This has led to natural growth in content-based commerce platforms of today. OHouse is one the nation's fastest growing apps and vertical commerce platforms, tripling in growth each year, with accrued trade topping 1 trillion won ($840 million) as of October 2020.

An alternative solution is for companies to collaborate with consumers from the product's initial planning phase to increase the points of contact with their clients. In other words, customers are actively taking the lead in the development of a product. Cosmetics powerhouse Amorepacific launched its Oversmudge Lip Tint line under its newest hip makeup brand Rarekind, as well as its line of edible collagen Soluderm, respectively in partnership with YouTube beauty content creator Minsco and influencer and radio show host Jihye Lee. These two celebrities took part in the development of the products, conveying questions from their viewers and followers, visiting the labs and manufacturing facilities, and taking part in skin tests and sharing results of their use of the products over a certain period. Such efforts to increase contact points with consumers can only lead to an enhanced interest in the goods even before their release.

Background to Like Commerce
— Enter an era of 24/7 shopping based on social media

Like Commerce's rise has led to an extensive expansion in connectivity, prompting companies to reconsider their approach to managing relations with customers. What companies need above all else at this moment is comprehensive business insight into the consumer-driven market. Let's look at the major catalysts in Like Commerce that prompted changes in the market. Everyone has at some point scrolled through eye-catching goods on social media feeds and community posts uploaded by friends and acquaintances. We are now less likely to buy products that appear in ads on television or in magazines. Uploads on social media are fast becoming the gateway to discovering products that we are interested in. We no longer take time from our lives to actually "go shopping" but rather make purchases anytime and anywhere through online searches or updated posts. And as such, consumers are putting in place new decision-making models that veer away from conventional norms.

If consumers previously bought products intentionally according to their needs, consumers now make purchases at any time after a chance encounter with some random video content. Buyers used to look up the products online once they notice them and then proceed with payment, prompting vendors to focus on beefing up their content on shopping platforms and online malls to make sure clients do not stray in the process. However, with shopping becoming an even more commonplace and regular part of our daily lives, companies need to develop enjoyable content to give heightened exposure of their products in a natural way that engenders a sense of empathy from customers. If the products garner recommendations prior to them coming in contact with the merchandise, it will surely induce customers to open their wallets.

The advent of a new generation with distinctive tastes

and consumer patterns has only served to maximize these new purchasing behaviors. Gen Zers, who are also digital natives, are more open to taking risks than the older generations and even enjoy this new paradigm of shopping. Furthermore, they have lower brand loyalty. The decision-making process of Like Commerce fits well with the tendencies of Gen Zers to prefer products that suit them best rather than luxury brands, and who also enjoy persuading and swaying others through YouTube and social media. They will likely lead the growth in Like Commerce as they emerge as key players in the consumer market. TikTok, the most favored social media platform among Gen Zers, has joined with Shopify and plans to follow other platforms and embed a shopping feature in its app. For consumers, Like Commerce will likely be a retail model of the future, as it coincides with our era of great transformation.

From a socioeconomic perspective, the rise of Like Commerce is inevitable. In a society where jobs are scarce and non-face-to-face interaction is obligatory, Like Commerce has become a viable alternate career and source of income. Rather than resting on their laurels relying on a fixed income, a growing number of people believe that it is wiser to accrue wealth by starting one's own business on the side. Opening an offline store is still too much of a risk during the pandemic and the ever-mounting financial woes it has caused small business owners. The one-person online opera-tion has become an appealing alternative.

Chronic issues in the Korean e-commerce market have also quickened the growth of Like Commerce. The Korean e-commerce market is overly dependent on shopping platforms compared to overseas businesses. If a manufacturer wishes to successfully launch its product, into which it has poured all its time, effort, and investment, the golden rule is to debut it on a giant e-commerce platform. The problem is that manufacturers have to meet any and all demands and conditions set by these platform operators. For example, exacerbating price wars between e-commerce platforms usually lead to manufacturers having to supply the goods at a lower cost. This inevitably results in dismal profit margins. Marketing strategy has also been a major problem. Any data on sales, purchase patterns, and their very own consumers are closely guarded by platform sites. Such an uneven playing field has only served to push manufacturers to seek their own sales channels.

Outlook and Implications
— A market that targets the individual buyer

Like Commerce is leading a change in the layout of online retail, but the outlook is far from a bed of roses. The spectacular growth conceals hidden thorns. Many consumers are weary of an endless succession of private enterprises popping up left and right, which is draining on marketing effectiveness and may cause a brand's value to tumble. If excessive competition prompts companies to churn out even more repetitive and mundane PR content, the brand and the vendor will lose reliability and trust. Moreover, profit margins at online malls operated by manufacturers in the D2C model are still somewhat limited, unless they are giant conglomerates with a higher brand value. So, what are the factors in Like Commerce that are vital for its future? We need to take a closer look at two elements, namely the consumer and sincerity, which can make or break a brand's success.

1. Focusing on the consumer: The "market of one"

Retail begins and ends with the consumer. Global business guru Ram Charan said in his book *Rethinking Competitive Advantage: New Rules for the Digital Age*, that one must focus on the consumer or "a market of one" to ensure a competitive edge in the digital age. He emphasizes that collecting data on consumers is essential to provide a level of personalization and hence better service. He points out that more data leads to better consumer insights; a larger scale generates more cash and enables better predictions that lead to more customer satisfaction and lower costs, which in turn increases revenue and cash gross margin, which provides the cash to innovate and ultimately serve the consumer better.

Streamlining existing external channels to better suit the needs of customers can be a wise strategy to outwardly encourage sales and to inwardly maximize personal experiences for customers. Here we should note Alibaba Group's example. The online commerce giant, which operates Tmall, China's largest e-commerce platform, opened "Luxury Pavilion" as part of Tmall's high-end sales operations in 2017. Luxury Pavilion made use of Alibaba's customer database and issued its exclusive access to the platform and invitations called "APASS," or Alibaba passports, to a choice group of clientele who had racked up top sales for Tmall as its highest spenders. If a buyer without any history of purchasing luxury brands logs on to Tmall, the platform shows products in the mid to low range. If an APASS holder logs on, Tmall shows the high-end luxury brands section on its mobile app and PC platform. This shows that even retail giants can figure out ways to make a more personalized shopping experience that meets a rising demand for exclusivity and customized experiences.

2. Sincerity: The key to communicative commerce

Compared to giant platforms, the greatest advantage unique to Like Commerce is the ability to initiate direct communication. To further emphasize Like Commerce's strength of competitiveness through communication, we can call it

"Communicative Commerce."

According to a report that analyzed live commerce in the first half of 2021 by MCN Leferi레페리, an agency that caters to about 280 beauty content creators and social media influencers and live streamers, between sessions that featured influencers as a one-off event and sessions that were part of an influencers' series and multiple appearances as a spokes-model for their product, average sales increased 21-fold for these multiple sessions compared with the one-off session. The content creators' direct participation in the market is effective and persuasive because they have already told their fans about the journey that was involved in planning, making, testing, and reviewing the product, thus giving fans time to get to know the product long before its launch. It is clear evidence that followers share an affinity with their favorite stars and influencers when they are sincere and give authentic reviews of their own products.

Like Commerce is a portent for major turmoil in para-digms for the retail industry. Its revolutionary nature itself may be significant, but it is more noteworthy that it is lead-ing a shift in the very core of consumer values. Customers are choosing "distinctive" products rather than "better" ones, moving from "different" to "best suited." Vendors need to keep in mind that consumers of today are more likely to tap "like" and proceed with payment for products that best suit them rather than "items that are better versions of the previous models, or those that are different from rival goods."

"What goods suit me best?" is a question that retailers of the future will have to answer.

Tell Me Your Narrative

Narratives hold great power. Armed with a narrative, a company with lackluster sales can see its share prices soar through the roof. A unique personal narrative helps focus public attention on politics or corporate branding. Narratives are unlike stories. Whereas stories emphasize recounting a series of events, narratives bring to the fore the storyteller's role of adding distinctive flair and creativity to the tale. If stories are about *what* is said, narratives are about *how* it is said.

In order for businesses to create a relatable narrative, they need to (a) display a mythos that appeals to emotions and symbolism; (b) create said mythos and narrative with a community of customers; (c) take a "universe" approach; and, for added effect, (d) add a dash of romance to the narrative for customers to fall in love with.

Leaders who can create a good narrative are able to captivate the masses. The unprecedented global outbreak of COVID-19 prompted concerns of an ever-widening spread of false narratives, making it increasingly difficult to discern true information from falsehood. We need to upgrade our sifting mechanisms or enhance our own abilities to detect and discard false narratives. Never before has it been more imperative to beef up our media literacy to help us independently analyze and critically accept information with a grain of salt. If the year 2022 is to serve as our springboard, we must ask ourselves, "What is my own narrative?"

The price-to-earnings ratio, more commonly referred to as the P/E ratio or PER, is often used by investors as a measure to evaluate a company's share prices in respect to its earnings per share. It determines the relative value of the shares vis-à-vis other companies or its own past track record. The PER of South Korea's benchmark KOSPI currently stands at around 11 or 12 times its annual earnings, and insiders say that if it dips below 12, it is undervalued, and if it goes higher, it is overvalued. Still, some companies that are not conforming to this formula are emerging in the market. Tesla, the Austin, Texas-based pioneer in the electric automobile industry, is a prime example. Its PER was well above 1,000 in the end of 2020 and first quarter of 2021. In other words, a buyer would have needed funds equivalent to about 1,000 times Tesla's annual net profit in order to purchase the company. Tesla is not alone. PERs for the big tech companies referred to as "FAANG," an acronym for Facebook (now Meta), Apple, Amazon, Netflix, and Google, as well as for Korean companies in the tech-heavy sectors known as "BBIG," short for battery, biotech, internet, and games, easily top 100.

In an attempt to rationalize such inexplicable figures, investors have created the term "PDR," or "price-to-dream ratio." Simply put, it is an indicator of a person's dream or wish. The term implies that pioneering firms whose share prices have soared after they managed to stand out as giants in new and rapidly growing business sectors need a new valuation system that takes into account their potential – in other words, their "dream factor." Companies that are opening the doors to an unparalleled market in which we are seeing exponential technological innovations such as artificial intelligence, autonomous mobility, and space exploration, can hardly be quantified through PER and other conventional means alone. Despite concerns that PDR is simply an indicator for a bubble in a company's stocks, hordes of investors are placing their bets on these dreams.

However, this does not mean that all promising firms have high PDRs. Only a select few are granted their dreams. So where do such "dreams" come from? Their roots lie in their narratives. Tesla did not rise to its heights simply by claiming that it wants "to make the world's best electric vehicle." Its CEO Elon Musk, often cited as the inspiration behind Robert Downey Jr.'s portrayal of Tony Stark in the Marvel movies, offered not just electric vehicles but a vision of autonomous cars that fully incorporated artificial intelligence and massive amounts of big data. Furthermore, he unveiled his blueprint for the future that included what he has dubbed "Neuralink," which involves computer chip implants in the brain that will allow users to directly communicate with and control their self-driving vehicles, as well as "The Boring Company," which would create a fast and efficient network of underground expressway tunnels beneath densely populated metropolises to help eliminate traffic congestion. This goes way beyond mere stories and becomes a narrative complete with a unique vision and worldview.

Narratives hold great power. The end of the COVID-19 pandemic comes not when we eradicate it. It ends when society accepts the narrative that "we can resume daily routines despite the virus." As our final chapter of *Consumer Trend Insights 2022*, we will outline what we have dubbed "Narrative Capital." Narratives bring people together and have the power to elicit action. We will take a closer look at what defines a narrative and what makes it wield such immense power.

What Forms a Narrative?

We are all familiar with the legendary tales of Isaac Newton formulating the law of gravity after seeing an apple fall from a tree, or of Archimedes and his "Eureka!" moment on volume and density after observing water spill over as he sat down in his bathtub. John D. Niles, an American scholar of medieval English literature who defined humanity as "narrative humans" in his 1999 work *Homo Narrans: The Poetics and Anthropology of Oral Literature*, noted that revelations in natural sciences seem to culminate in interesting narratives about academic achievements. Every aspect of this world begins and ends with the narrative, with countless religions and their feast of expansive narratives extending their reach to all corners of the world. As such, narratives are instinctive and basic requisites for human communication.

The etymology of "narrative" comes from the Latin word "*narrare*," meaning to describe or to relate, which in turn derives from "*gnarus* (having knowledge of)" and "*narro* (to make known)." It is not simply an act of telling but also implies the aim of attaining knowledge. In other words, a narrative does not simply recount a series of occurrences – it injects meaning into the world and shows what significance a narrative has on our lives.

The Merriam-Webster dictionary defines "narrative" as "a way of presenting or understanding a situation or series of events that reflects and promotes a particular point of view or set of values." Whereas a story focuses on "what is said," the crux of a narrative lies in "how the story is structured and conveyed." Namely, if the former refers to the actual content, the latter pertains to how it is styled and conveyed. For example, the discourse on the American Dream or

	Storytelling	Narrative
Methodology	Conveying a tale	Interpretive communication
Development	Series of events	Strategy of structured discourse
Structure	Linear	Open & cyclical
Goals	Personal interest	Social value
Conclusion	Conclusion within text	Completed with audience
Focus	Content and conclusion	Process and method
Flow	Passage of time	Beyond time & space

Sinocentrism中華思想 is not just a collection of stories but encompasses a narrative. This is because it is a perspective on the world – a comprehensive concept that affects the ideology and decision-making process. We can summarize the features and differences between narratives and storytelling in the chart above.

The Need for a Business Narrative

Here is a tale of two retailers. Retailer A posted annual sales of 17 trillion won ($15.7 billion) and an operating profit of 427 billion won ($395 million), while Retailer B saw revenue of 7 trillion won ($6.5 billion) and an operating loss of 720.5

billion won ($665 million). Which retailer has more enterprise value (EV)?

The answer is Retailer B. Whereas Retailer A is an affiliate of a large-scale conglomerate, Retailer B was Coupang. If we were to take a cursory glance at performance figures, Retailer A would seem to have the upper hand. However, Retailer B took the lead by an overwhelming margin in terms of EV. Coupang's EV was estimated at 69 trillion won ($61 billion) when it was listed on the New York Stock Exchange in March 2021, astounding many in the industry as well as investors and financial firms. The outcome simply was irrational and inexplicable. Coupang's narrative had exceeded the limitations of its performance.

Narratives strongly reflect corporate and economic valuation in the market. Investors are looking at and examining how companies have grown, their track records, and their future potential and value to gauge their EVs. Designing a business narrative strategy is now no longer a choice but an imperative in the corporate sector.

Conventional means of corporate evaluation and measuring stock price values are also changing. As we shift from a labor- and capital-centric hardware economy toward a software economy, narratives about corporate culture, branding, customer relations, and the competency of executives and employees are emerging as major elements that affect EVs. We are living in an era of new valuation methods for economic indicators. Narrative factors have become particularly crucial in the investment sector. This is attributed to investors who are seeking to find companies with appealing narratives, rather than simply focusing on the numbers. Even analysts and investment strategists are trying to imbue their analytical data with meaningful narratives.

Investors often use the term "total addressable market (TAM)" to quantify the relevant total market size and gauge what we referred to earlier as "PDR," the price-to-dream ratio. They multiply TAM with the company's market share and divide it by the company's total market capitalization. The problem is that quantifying total market size can be quite subjective. The EV for Tesla can be based on the electric vehicle market estimated at $100 trillion. But if we are to include in the equation Elon Musk's other innovative ventures such as SpaceX, Starlink, The Boring Company, and Robotaxi, Tesla's PDR grows exponentially. The narrative has the power to nudge people to believe and invest in the dream. As a result, the company's share price will continue to rise, even if it posts dismal profits or even a net loss. This is because investors are placing their bets on the future narrative of success.

A narrative is also vital in establishing a new economic structure or concept. The key example is cryptocurrency, namely Bitcoin. From a traditional economic perspective, Bitcoin is literally and figuratively quite cryptic. Bitcoin does not have an intrinsic value, according to economic standards, because it is purely a computer algorithm. There are no interests or dividends, it is not easily exchangeable for gold, and payments with it are not backed by a central bank. Still, Bitcoin's value has skyrocketed. Why? The narrative is also a driving force behind its explosive rise in value.

Bitcoin was reportedly created in 2008 by an anonymous developer who wrote a paper under the moniker of Satoshi Nakamoto. Its narrative begins from a distrust of the centralized financial system after the subprime mortgage meltdown and ensuing global financial crisis in 2007. So, here we have all the elements of an anti-authoritarian anarchist narrative – the mysterious hero fighting against a corrupt nation and its authorities in a plot that seems straight out of a detective novel – which has a mythical, even romantic, appeal that resonates with the public. As a matter of fact, Bitcoin is entirely controlled by anonymous users around the world, and thus, in theory, is free from government regulation or any other powerful oversight. Such heroic tales have spawned other narratives of the average Joe striking it rich overnight, further amplifying and propagating narrative's power and lure. On February 9, 2021, when Tesla announced that it had bought $1.5 billion in Bitcoin, its prices shot up. Elon Musk's singular image as "an icon of the future" had driven up the value, as though he was a prophet or a super spreader of the Bitcoin narrative. And adding to this was yet another appealing narrative of "taking part in the future," further amplifying the effect and resulting in endless price fluctuations.

Strategies for a Business Narrative

The world of business is where narrative capital has proven most effective, especially in terms of marketing and corporate branding. A well-structured narrative can wield enormous power in effective marketing and in establishing brands. This is because establishing brands and business models is very similar to writing stories. Creating a solid brand narrative itself becomes an irreplaceable epic. Rivals can outwardly imitate snippets of the business strategy but can never imitate a unique narrative. This grants an overwhelming and unprecedented market share for the brand.

The birth of an irreplaceable brand narrative is only possible when the company has a unique quality. However, most firms' origin stories and marketing campaigns appear quite similar and rather commonplace. Then how can businesses create a unique and dominating brand that sets it apart from other bland, average, and monotonous ones? What kind of strategy can they apply to maximize their narrative capital in their sector?

1. From logos to mythos

If a narrative is to have any power, companies must target the mythos rather than the logos. Where logos pertains to logic and reason, mythos appeals to emotion and symbolism. Unlike logos, the language of truth and logic, mythos is a language of legends that conjures collective memories from a distant past. Narratives grow even stronger when they are based in their original literary and artistic myths. The audience is more naturally drawn to mythos than to logos.

Take for instance the change of seasons. In terms of logos, it can be explained logically by referencing the tilted axis of the rotating earth. However, from a mythical perspective, its reasons are more complex, involving the lovelorn Hades, the God of the underworld, who abducted Persephone, the beloved daughter of Demeter, goddess of the harvest. Struck by grief, Demeter denied the growth and production of all life on earth, causing catastrophic famine. Beset by the cries of hunger and pleas from the people, Zeus, the father of Persephone, ordered his brother Hades to return Persephone to her mother. But because Hades had tricked her to eat some pomegranate seeds before her departure, Persephone had to return to Hades' side for one third of the year, spending the remaining two-thirds with her mother above the surface. And thus we have to endure the cold winter months when Persephone leaves her mother's side for the underworld, creating the cycle of seasons.

When narratives meet mythical reasons, they become a force to be reckoned with. It may be less than logical and quite unconvincing, but it acts as a great source of motivation that piques the people's interest. Mythos possesses such supernatural mythical power. In our modern world dominated by logos, marketing through mythmaking becomes essential in creating legendary brands that create emotional values and dreams, as well as a way of life. Brands that are rooted in mythical origins can directly convey embodied emotions and philosophies to their customers.

Truth be told, imbedding a mythical narrative in a brand is a classic strategy. Evian, considered a pioneer in the bottled water market, is rooted in a mythical message associated with health, youth, beauty, and fitness. It branded its origins to the French Alps, with rain and snowfall mixing with the perpetual snow of the slopes, which is then filtered by a subterranean aquifer for fifteen years or more, resulting in natural spring water rich in minerals from the glacial sand. Legend has it that the springs were discovered in 1789 by Marquis de Lessert, who was suffering from debilitating pain caused by kidney stones. When traveling through the spa town of Évian-les-Bains, famed for its thermal springs, he drank from the natural water welling up in the garden of his lodgings. This was known as "taking the waters" in those days, a widely accepted practice of bathing or drinking water thought to be good for one's health. His pain miraculously subsided and he found that his kidney stones were cured – presumably because they passed through his system. Word of the water's purportedly miraculous healing properties spread like wildfire, drawing an endless stream of ailing people to the town, with some doctors prescribing the water as a cure. Even Napoleon III reportedly favored the water of Évian. In 1878, l'Académie française de médecine, now known as l'Académie nationale de médecine, gave its official stamp of approval to the waters, recognizing its beneficial properties. Such a brand narrative spread quickly by word of mouth, especially among the well-to-do elite who often spent their holidays by the shores of Lake Geneva, helping its initial recognition as a luxury item for the rich and famous which provided an opportunity to corner an untapped market at the time.

Gabrielle Bonheur Chanel, creator of one of the world's first luxury brands, is a legend of haute couture. Her brand is rooted in her legendary narrative which has maintained its rich aura for more than a century. Many people note that her stylings gave women "freedom of movement," as she eliminated the need for corsets and gave them pants and skirts that only reached their knees rather than full-length dresses that only dragged and restricted them, which were still the mainstream fashion in the early 20th century. Born in 1883, her mother died when she was 11 and her father, a peddler, sent her and her two sisters to a convent where nuns taught her to sew, which would become the basis of her lifelong career. She took the stage name of "Coco" during her brief career as a singer in her late teens and early twenties while also working a second job as a sales assistant. Starting as a milliner, she opened her own hugely successful hat boutique in Paris in 1910 and then another in Deauville, a popular holiday destination for the rich and famous. When she branched out into high fashion in 1916, ladies were still encased in corsets and crinoline, which Chanel found cumbersome and restricting. She shortened the length of the dresses, designed trousers for women, and attached straps to handbags and purses so that they could be worn on the shoulder. Her attempts became innovations that broke with stereotypes and allowed the brand to represent female empowerment and women's liberation.

2. Creating a narrative with the community of customers

Companies need to learn how to do away with antiquated methods and mannerisms and reset the stage for the game if they hope to attain a unique brand narrative. The role of their customers becomes crucial in this endeavor. In 2019, Musinsa, a relative newcomer among retailers, joined an exclusive group of unicorn companies, or non-listed startups with valuations of more than $1 billion. The fashion platform focuses on content created by their own customers. Its roots lie in a social-club/community web site, with its name stemming from an acronym for "a place with tons of photos of shoes무진장 신발 사진이 많은 곳." Neither its managers nor executives can infringe on the company's store rankings which is created spontaneously by its fans. Their policies have only served to instill loyalty among their customers, prompting them to stay longer on their site and contribute to content that directly leads to sales. Its very corporate identity is being defined by the content created by the client community itself. Working closely with its community to complete its uniquely spontaneous narrative is clearly evident as Musinsa's business strategy. And in such narrative branding, the concept of a "community" comes to the fore, rather than that of an "audience."

When creating a brand narrative, establishing a strong fandom for the community of customers becomes crucial. ARMY, the mighty fandom for global pop sensation BTS, conducted a fan-driven census in 2020 to mark its 7th anniversary. It sought to address stereotypes and reveal the exact makeup of the global fanbase and analyze the data into quantifiable numbers. The 10-question census was translated into more than 40 languages and posted on an independent site between July 9 and September 30, 2020, drawing responses from some 400,000 fans in more than 100 countries and territories across the globe. The analysts, who also included Bangtan Scholars, a community of scholars, researchers, professors, and statisticians, collated the data and announced the results in early 2021. While the organizers admit that their census is merely a snapshot and does not represent 100% of the fandom's millions, the results showed that the fanbase consisted of more than just teenagers. The census did show that nearly 87% of respondents were indeed women, but also that just over half were teenagers. Those between the ages of 18 and 29 constitute more than 42% of respondents, while roughly 7% were those in their 30s, 40s, 50s, and even over 60. A quick search of "BTS" and "ARMY" hashtags on social media and YouTube shows fans across all races, genders, generations, and professions, talking about how they came across the group, BTS's appeal, and why they have such an affinity with the septet, their songs, and messages. This is a prime example of a brand narrative in which fandoms voluntarily create and determine their own identity.

3. Narrative within a universe

Another modern narrative strategy is the "fictional universe" approach. In this universe, magic, superluminal speed, and other elements of fantasy and science fiction play out against a backdrop of an imaginary city, nation, or planet. We can count *The Lord of the Rings* and *Star Wars* series as clear examples, but none more so than the superhero mega franchise known as the Marvel Cinematic Universe, or MCU, which is creating what is equivalent to modern day myths and legends. None of its movies tells a simple, standalone tale but rather they affect and in turn are affected by others in the same universe, continuously expanding its worldview and spawning countless spinoffs and derivative content in a transmedia narrative that encompasses books, films, radio, television, video games, and even theme parks. The vast universe created through sprawling collective narratives churns out endless content to meet the exacting demands of their loyal and raving audience and to reach out to new ones.

Such a "universal" approach is not exclusive to cinema. The music industry has embraced elements of the strategy. BTS is also creating a global and detailed universe narrative with content that is related to the BTS Universe featuring its BU logo. Such narratives do not necessarily unfold chronologically but rather are scattered throughout their content, like individual pieces to a puzzle. The BTS ARMY are famous for analyzing the music videos frame by frame, hunting down each and every puzzle piece, further motivated by repetitive elements that reappear, offering their own interpretations on how it all fits together.

4. The triangle and the romantic narrative

Everyone loves a romance story. Companies couldn't be happier if they are able to induce clients to fall in love with their brands. In fact, most marketing is a form of courtship. So how can companies create a romantic narrative to entice their customers to fall head over heels for their brands?

American psychologist Robert Sternberg, renowned for his "triangular theory of love," claims that love is composed of three components: intimacy, passion, and decision/commitment, which forms the three sides of a triangle. This can also be construed as a romantic narrative triangle. If a firm evenly satisfies all three elements, it will be able to create a perfectly balanced triangle that equally blends emotional attachment with rational logic. When a passionate fandom takes part in writing a brand narrative and thereby expressing their intimate love for the brand, they create a cult brand that has a devoted and committed following.

A strategy to personify products and services can prove effective in finalizing this brand romance. The most common form is that of character marketing, whereby the company creates a narrative in which consumers can relate to a specific character for which they establish an affinity, thereby becoming more familiar with the related brand. Creating a personal bond between the brand and consumers helps to establish empathy and emotional interactions.

Characters that became famous in marketing campaigns have even become the names of some companies. Case in point, Lotte Group. Its name comes from the female character Charlotte in Goethe's best-known romantic work *Die Leiden des jungen Werthers* (*The Sorrows of Young Werther*). The late Shin Kyuk-ho, who founded Lotte Group, was reportedly so enamored by the short story that he named his company after her, which allowed the firm to convey a narrative of romance imbued in its origins. Lotte Group even named its theater specializing in musicals the "Charlotte Theater샤롯데씨어터," and also commissioned a statue of Goethe to stand in the plaza for its 123-story Lotte World Tower, the fifth-tallest building in the world and the tallest in the nation. With its humble roots as a chewing gum manufacturer, then later branching out into confectionery, retail, construction, and chemicals, Lotte now leans more to the heavy industries. Nevertheless, the literary and romantic narrative conjured by the name "Lotte" has not changed.

What is important is that the romantic narrative must remain consistent, regardless of whether it is triangular or involves a character. Companies need to consider the concept of standardization when establishing a brand narrative, which is a process to inject coherency and continuity to events that appear to be disorderly. Setting proper standards helps establish a clear narrative and enhances cogency and validity. Therefore, it is vital for firms to maintain consistency and unity in their narratives.

COVID-19 and Fake News

The unique nature of COVID-19 has given rise to various

crises in our society, one of which is cause for particular concern: a narrative crisis. We all face a crisis of faith, one in which we are wary and find it more and more difficult to trust one another, which has engendered a breeding ground for fake narratives. Raging epidemics in the past bred fear and false rumors that spread like wildfire. Social trust is collapsing, with false information fueling chaos and confusion. Nobel Prize winning Yale economist Robert J. Shiller, in his 2019 book *Narrative Economics: How Stories Go Viral and Drive Major Economic Events*, describes how narratives can go viral, much like the spread of an epidemic. We can apply the model of epidemic contagion to that of narratives, and the two can even jointly spread at the same pace, sometimes feeding off each other. Fake narratives grow stronger and spread even faster than truths. According to an article published in Science magazine in 2018, tweets containing false information were 70% more likely to be retweeted than truthful ones.

Moreover, SARS-CoV-2 is an unprecedented contagion that for many remains a mystery. Lack of information led false information to go unchecked, leading to an information infection. The outbreak of the coronavirus led to the "infodemic," a portmanteau of "information" and "pandemic," which the World Health Organization defines as the propagation of excessive information, false or misleading, in all forms of media including digital, the press, or broadcasting. Also referred to as "fake news," the infodemic flared up in areas that saw the highest concentration of the viral outbreak, and later reproduced itself through translations that broadened its reach into other countries.

So, how detrimental is the scope of fake news? The basic reproduction number, or R_0, indicates how contagious an infectious disease is as it gauges the average number of secondary infections caused by one infected individual. If the R_0 for the contagion is smaller than 1, it should gradually recede. The Institute for Complex Systems, which operates under Italy's National Research Council, analyzed in March 2020 the R_0 of fake news through a transmission prediction mathematical model. It focused on 1.3 million posts, tweets, and uploads, as well as 7.5 million threads and comments on five major social media platforms, including Twitter, YouTube, and Instagram, and determined an R_0 of 3.3. The R_0 for Instagram alone measured at a whopping 130. In contrast, the R_0 for the actual virus itself stood at 2.0 to 2.5. It became clear that false information was spreading quickly through social media along with verified facts and news.

The accelerated pace of the digital era has also prompted concerns of a lopsided narrative. The advances in information technology have allowed access to a vast stream of data which can easily become an unmanageable deluge. False information that spreads through social media only serves to speed up online confirmation bias. We mistakenly assume that information attained through the internet allows us to have an open perspective and accept diverse opinions, when in fact it is all too easy to form warped ideas and biased views. This is because we can simply cocoon ourselves in our comfortable "echo chambers," to accept news that only suit our preconceived notions.

Amid a rapid pace of development in technology, it is becoming more and more difficult to sift through the influx of information to discern truths from fake news. In the end, we will need to upgrade our sifting mechanisms or enhance our own abilities to detect and discard false narratives. In an age where digital literacy has become imperative, we must improve our media literacy to help us independently analyze and critically accept information with a grain of salt.

Outlook and Implications
— Ask yourself: "What Is my own narrative?"

We no longer live in an age where a company's valuation can simply be quantified through conventional economic measurements. The corporate valuation of today rests on whether it possesses a singular business model, or if it has a creative entrepreneurial spirit, and whether it can provide a clear vision for the future. Even if they do not immediately post definitive profit, a company's future may rest on whether its CEO can present a blueprint with near-infinite potential. Businesses may have to take a page from Marvel flicks, with their chief executives displaying their superpowers and creating unique narratives that encompass their corporate values and philosophies. We have entered an age where companies are selling not just products, but also dreams.

Therefore, it is no longer possible to copycat a brand identity. Firms must carefully consider their core values and draw up a meticulous structural plot to create a brand narrative with an unshakeable identity. Establishing such identities will inspire loyal fans and foster a fandom that lends a hand in writing the narrative.

This year will see back-to-back elections to choose South Korea's president as well as regional government leaders. Candidates that successfully make effective use of narratives will have a decided advantage. As investors readily pour astronomical sums of investment into future potential, voters are more likely to be drawn to those who make a convincing case for a relatable future. Their narratives will be even more potent if candidates can convey a frank and sincere portrayal of their life stories, laying bare their strengths and weaknesses, then make a natural segue into sincere political discourse, allowing them to win over their constituents.

As we previously outlined, narratives are rooted in infinite imagination, touching on creativity. We live in a world where those who manage to achieve and accomplish feats that everyone thought impossible or ludicrous become the ultimate winners. We may initially think they live in a far-off distant world, but we often find that their "ludicrous" dreams are right on our doorstep. We are smitten by their mesmerizing narrative. What is the source for such entrancing tales?

Perhaps we are always searching for our unadulterated selves from lost childhoods who were filled with imagination. Our senses may have dulled, and our once boundless curiosity may have waned as we live day to day steeped in convention. You may recall the opening scene from *Alice's Adventures in Wonderland*, in which Alice, who was initially weary of her monotonous life, hurries after an obviously flustered White Rabbit – wearing a waistcoat and looking at a pocket watch, no less – and chases him down a rabbit hole and into Wonderland. It may be that we all yearn for a narrative similar to that of Alice and live a life full of adventure and wonder. Creating brand-new narratives will be impossible if we are bogged down by rules and conventions. If the year 2022 is to serve as our springboard, we must ask ourselves, "What is my own narrative?"

2022
Consumer Trend Insights

초판 1쇄 발행 2022년 2월 15일

지은이 김난도, 전미영, 최지혜, 이향은, 이준영, 이수진,
　　　　서유현, 권정윤, 한다혜, 이혜원, 추예린
번역 구희진
감수 미셸 램블린
펴낸이 성의현
펴낸곳 (주)미래의창

출판 신고 2019년 10월 28일 제2019-000291호
주소 서울시 마포구 잔다리로 62-1 미래의창빌딩(서교동 376-15, 5층)
전화 070-8693-1719 **팩스** 0507-1301-1585
홈페이지 www.miraebook.co.kr
ISBN 978-89-5989-702-5　13320

생각이 글이 되고, 글이 책이 되는 놀라운 경험. 미래의창과 함께라면 가능합니다.
책을 통해 여러분의 생각과 아이디어를 더 많은 사람들과 공유하시기 바랍니다.
투고메일 togo@miraebook.co.kr (홈페이지와 블로그에서 양식을 다운로드하세요)
제휴 및 기타 문의 ask@miraebook.co.kr